Winner's! ENGLISH

Basic Lessons For Portuguese Speakers

**BOOK 1
Lessons 1 - 20**

Winner's! ENGLISH

Winner's! English Books
No unauthorized reproduction

winnersenglishbooks@gmail.com

All rights reserved. No part of this publication may be reproduced, stored in a retrieval system, or transmitted, in any form or by any means, without the prior permission in writing of Winner's English Books.

This book is sold subject to the condition that it shall not, by the way of trade or otherwise, be lent, resold, hired out, or otherwise circulated without the publisher's prior consent in any form of binding or cover than that in which it is published and without a similar condition including this condition being imposed on the subsequent purchaser.

Copyright © 2021
All rights reserved.

ISBN: 9798459159783

These lessons are part of the series:

"Winner's! English – Basic Lessons For Portuguese Speakers"
Book 1 (Lessons 1 – 20) +
Book 2 (Lessons 21 – 40)

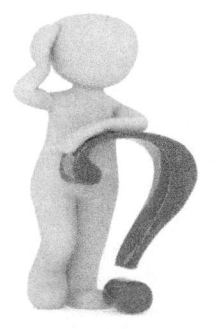

Do you know...?

Numbers números

one 1	two 2	three 3	four 4	five 5
six 6	seven 7	eight 8	nine 9	ten 10
eleven 11	twelve 12	thirteen 13	fourteen 14	fifteen 15
sixteen 16	seventeen 17	eighteen 18	nineteen 19	twenty 20

Days of the week dias da semana

Monday, Tuesday, Wednesday, Thursday, Friday, Saturday, Sunday

Useful Questions

How do you spell X? Como se soletra X?
What does X mean? O que X quer dizer?
How do you say X in English? Como é que se diz X em Inglês?

CONTENTS

Lesson 1: My pencil case meu estojo de lapis	Page 1
Lesson 2: In the classroom na sala de aula	Page 7
Lesson 3: My family minha família	Page 13
Lesson 4: Shapes formas	Page 19
Lesson 5: At the toy store na loja de brinquedos	Page 25
TEST 1	Page 31
Lesson 6: Food & drinks alimentos e bebidas	Page 33
Lesson 7: Vegetables legumes	Page 39
Lesson 8: Colors as cores	Page 45
Lesson 9: At the fruit market mercado de frutas	Page 51
Lesson 10: Feelings sentimentos	Page 57
TEST 2	Page 63
Lesson 11: At the zoo no jardim zoológico	Page 65
Lesson 12: Clothes roupas	Page 71
Lesson 13: Countries países	Page 77
Lesson 14: Places locais	Page 83
Lesson 15: Transportation transporte	Page 89
TEST 3	Page 95
Lesson 16: Meats carnes	Page 97
Lesson 17: At school na escola	Page 103
Lesson 18: More clothes mais roupas	Page 109
Lesson 19: More places mais lugares	Page 115
Lesson 20: The weather o tempo	Page 121
TEST 4	Page 127
TEST Answers	Page 129

Lesson 1: My pencil case

meu estojo de lapis

Part 1A: Learn the words

1. **a pencil**
   lapis
2. **a pen**
   caneta
3. **some glue**
   cola
4. **a ruler**
   régua
5. **a pencil sharpener**
   apontador de lápis
6. **an eraser**
   borracha
7. **some whiteout**
   corretivo líquido
8. **some tape**
   fita
9. **a marker**
   marcador
10. **a crayon**
    giz de cera

⭐ Practice speaking: "_Lapis_" is "_pencil_" in English! ⭐

Part 1B: Write the words

Write the missing letters!   Write x 1   Write x 2

1. __e__c__l   pencil _____   _____
2. p__n   _____   _____
3. __l__e   _____   _____
4. r__l__r   _____   _____
5. __e__c__l __h__rp__ner _____   _____
6. __r__s__r   _____   _____
7. w__i__e__u__   _____   _____
8. __a__e   _____   _____
9. m__r__e__   _____   _____
10. __r__y__n   _____   _____

1

Part 2A: Ask a question

What is <u>this</u>?

✓ **This** is <u>a pencil</u>. It is not <u>a pen</u>.

What is <u>that</u>?

✓ **That** is <u>a crayon</u>. It isn't <u>a marker</u>.

★ **Winner's Tip!** isn't = is not

Part 2B: Fill in the blanks

1. What is _____?
   This _____ a ruler. _____ isn't _____.

2. _____ is that?
   _____ is _____. It isn't _____.

3. _____ is _____?
   That _____ some glue. It _____ _____.

4. _____ is _____?
   This is _____. _____ _____ some whiteout.

Part 3A: Yes / No questions

Is <u>this</u> <u>a pencil sharpener</u>?

✓ **Yes, it is. This is** a pencil sharpener.
✗ **No, it isn't. This isn't** a pencil sharpener.

Is <u>that</u> <u>some tape</u>?

✓ **Yes, it is. That is** some tape.
✗ **No, it isn't. That isn't** some tape.

⭐ **Winner's Tip!** Important: this / that

Part 3B: Fill in the blanks

1. Is this _____?
   Yes, it _____. This _____ _____.

2. _____ that _____?
   No, _____ isn't. _____ isn't _____.

3. _____ this _____?
   No, _____ _____. _____ isn't _____.

4. Is _____ _____?
   Yes, _____ is. That _____ _____.

Part 4A: Verb of the day

buy / buys – bought – buying – bought (comprar)

Every month, I <u>buy</u> a new eraser.

On weekends, he <u>buys</u> pencils and pens.

Yesterday, we <u>bought</u> some new glue.

He is <u>buying</u> some whiteout right now.

I have never <u>bought</u> a good ruler.

Part 4B: Verb Practice

1. Every Saturday, I _____ a new pen.
2. On Thursdays, she _____ markers and tape.
3. Every year, he _____ a new pencil sharpener.
4. Last night, they _____ a few pencils.
5. Last week, I _____ a great new marker.
6. Yesterday, you _____ two rulers.
7. Right now, he is _____ some glue.
8. They are _____ ten crayons right now.
9. I have never _____ a great pencil case.
10. We have _____ pens from that store many times.

Part 5A: Phonics Practice

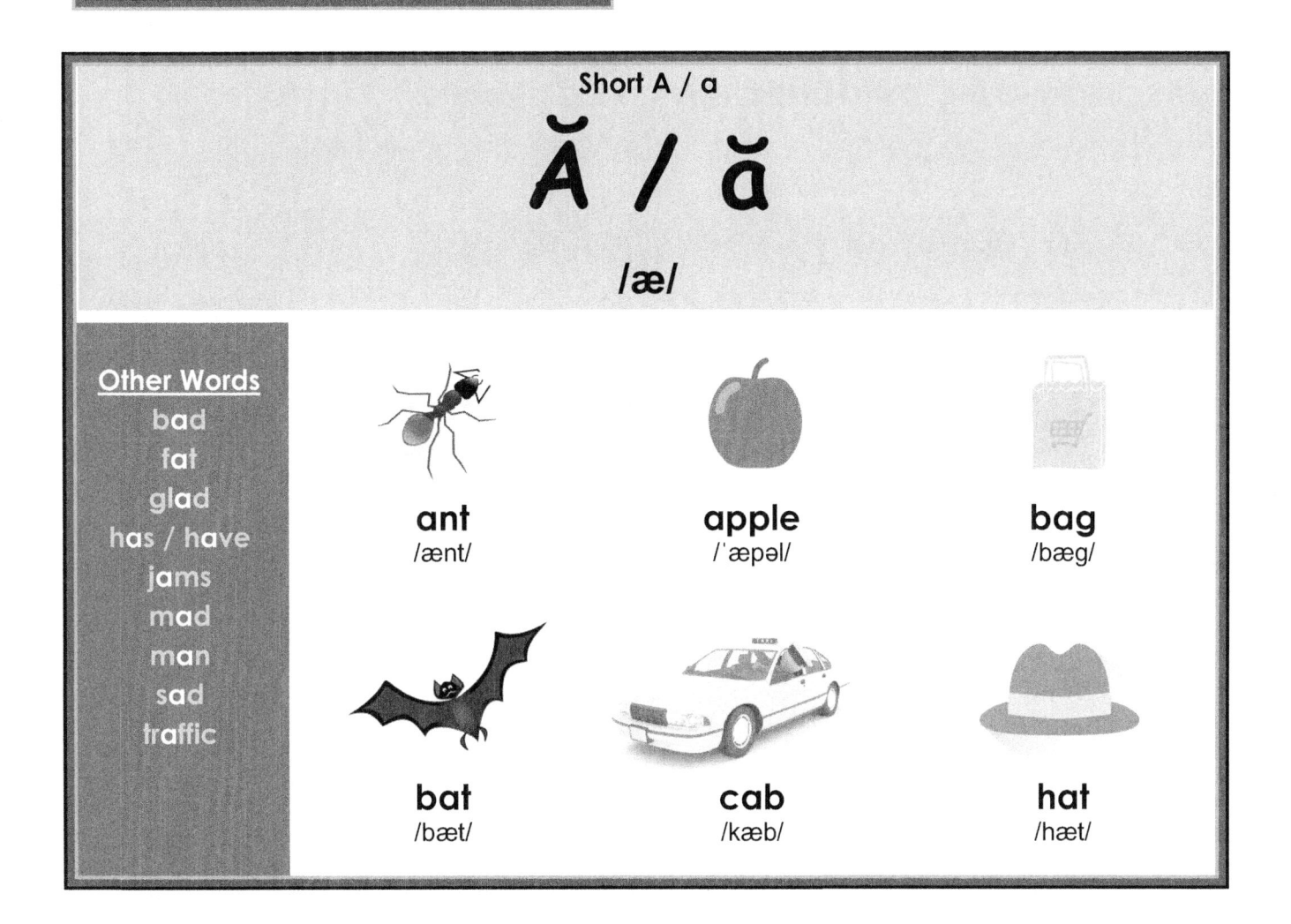

Short A / a
Ă / ă
/æ/

Other Words
bad
fat
glad
has / have
jams
mad
man
sad
traffic

ant
/ænt/

apple
/ˈæpəl/

bag
/bæg/

bat
/bæt/

cab
/kæb/

hat
/hæt/

Part 5B: Write and read

1. Gl__d h__t m__n h__s s__d b__ts.

2. __pple b__gs h__ve f__t __nts.

3. B__d c__bs h__ve m__d tr__ffic j__ms.

Part 6: Fun review

Unscramble the words and match

What did you buy for your pencil case?

npe _____pen_____
sarere _____
cnlpei _____
ienpcl rpnheears _____
lerur _____
ptea _____
rkemra _____
oycarn _____

What did you not buy for your pencil case?

ulge _____
tutiohwe _____
I didn't buy _____ and _____.

Lesson 2: In the classroom

na sala de aula

Part 1A: Learn the words

1. **blackboard**
   quadro-preto
2. **book**
   livro
3. **bookshelf**
   estante
4. **chair**
   cadeira
5. **clock**
   relógio
6. **computer**
   computador
7. **desk**
   a secretaria
8. **globe**
   globo
9. **poster**
   poster
10. **whiteboard**
    quadro branco

⭐ Practice speaking: "_Cadeira_" is "_chair_" in English! ⭐

Part 1B: Write the words

Write the missing letters!   Write x 1   Write x 2

1. b _ a _ k _ o _ r _
2. _ o _ k
3. b _ o _ s _ e _ f
4. _ h _ i _
5. c _ o _ k
6. _ o _ p _ t _ r
7. d _ s _
8. _ l _ b _
9. p _ s _ e _
10. _ h _ t _ b _ a _ d

Part 2A: Ask a question

What are these?

✓ **These** are <u>books</u>. They are not <u>computers</u>.

What are those?

✓ **Those** are <u>whiteboards</u>. They aren't <u>blackboards</u>.

★ **Winner's Tip!** aren't = are not

Part 2B: Fill in the blanks

1. What are _____?
   These _____ posters. _____ aren't _____.

2. _____ are those?
   _____ are _____. They _____ _____.

3. _____ are _____?
   These _____ bookshelves. They _____ _____.

4. _____ are _____?
   Those are _____. _____ _____ _____.

Part 3A: Yes / No questions

Are these clocks?

✓ **Yes, they are.** These are clocks.
✗ **No, they aren't.** These aren't clocks.

Are those globes?

✓ **Yes, they are.** Those are globes.
✗ **No, they aren't.** Those aren't globes.

⭐ **Winner's Tip!** Important: these / those

Part 3B: Fill in the blanks

1. Are these _____?
   Yes, they _____. They _____ _____.

2. _____ those _____?
   No, _____ aren't. _____ aren't _____.

3. _____ these _____?
   No, _____ _____. _____ aren't _____.

4. Are _____ _____?
   Yes, _____ are. Those _____ _____.

Part 4A: Verb of the day

look / looks – looked – looking – looked (olhar)

Every morning, I <u>look</u> at the blackboard.

On Fridays, she <u>looks</u> at the clock.

Yesterday, we <u>looked</u> at some posters.

She is <u>looking</u> at the bookshelf now.

I have never <u>looked</u> at his desk.

Part 4B: Verb Practice

1. Every Monday, I _____ for my books.
2. On Wednesdays, she _____ at her computer.
3. Every Sunday, he _____ for places on his globe.
4. Last class, they _____ at the blackboard.
5. Last weekend, I _____ for a new desk for my room.
6. This morning, we _____ on the bookshelf.
7. Right now, he is _____ under the chair.
8. We are _____ in the classroom right now.
9. She has never _____ at the whiteboard before.
10. You have _____ at your computer all day.

Part 5A: Phonics Practice

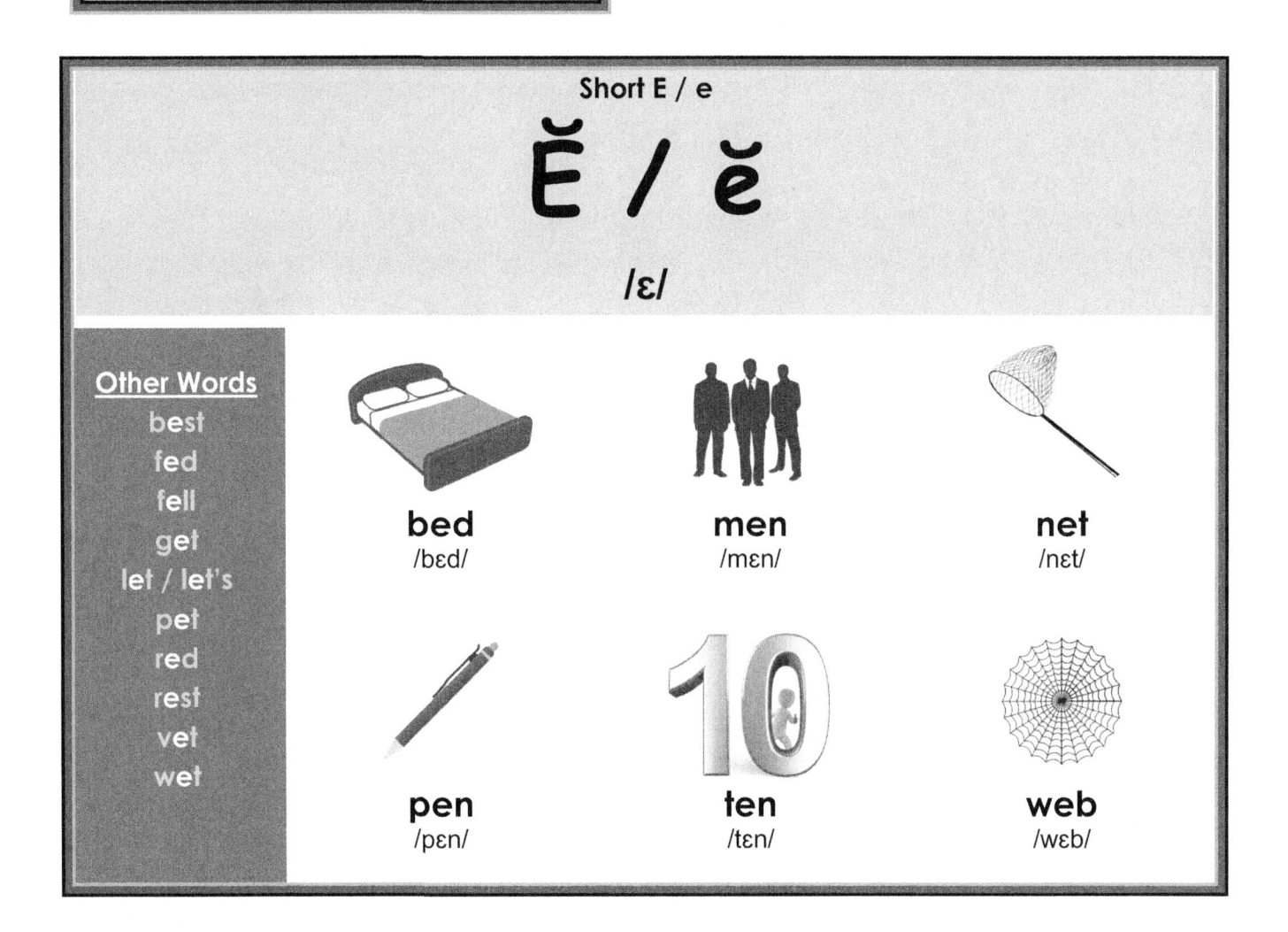

Short E / e

Ĕ / ĕ

/ɛ/

Other Words
best
fed
fell
get
let / let's
pet
red
rest
vet
wet

bed /bɛd/

men /mɛn/

net /nɛt/

pen /pɛn/

ten /tɛn/

web /wɛb/

Part 5B: Write and read

1. R__d n__ts f__ll on b__st m__n.
2. W__t v__ts l__t f__d p__ts g__t r__st.
3. L__t's g__t t__n w__b p__ns.

Part 6: Fun review

Find the words

```
l a n y p b y d l e r c c l m g v w e o
w r x f q g u l a f u i g l o b e g s s
i u p g f b i r b c c e v y s d h w z b
n o l o p o x y e b l a c k b o a r d n
n b k a d a s h g z f j r y p f z i h r
e m k s j m l b s r c e i f t p l n t s
r l w f f y m o f t t g u x f n k t x v
s m h k v y z o q s m x c h a i r h k o
e e i e m x w k o o p d b h b d a e s w
n p t v t p y p i y x o n e o y h c w e
g b e b l n o j x t r m w x o w j l u z
l r b x n b l j e c c l o c k d k a y q
i m o x w w k o r o o j u z s f r s d v
s x a i j w x z u m b r h u h f m s q m
h r r a u u h i n p s o d k e b e r w a
u p d k u r t o h u k p e h l a h o a j
v f s a m t v b k t j v s q f b b o v f
w f y w w b g x b e w p k u o w n m l o
n g t n k o s o h r c p i o p b d t i s
k h f p a y z t w m g u f l a g c g o c
```

chair	whiteboard
blackboard	desk
poster	bookshelf
globe	computer
clock	book

Lesson 3: My family

minha família

Part 1A: Learn the words

1. **mother**
   mãe
2. **sister**
   irmã
3. **aunt**
   tia
4. **cousin**
   prima / primo
5. **grandmother**
   avó
6. **father**
   pai
7. **brother**
   irmão
8. **uncle**
   tio
9. **niece / nephew**
   sobrinha / sobrinho
10. **grandfather**
    avô

⭐ Practice speaking: "_Mãe_" is "_mother_" in English! ⭐

Part 1B: Write the words

Write the missing letters!   Write x 1   Write x 2

1. m _ t _ e _
2. s _ s _ e _
3. _ u _ t
4. c _ u _ i _
5. g _ a _ d _ ot _ er
6. _ a _ h _ r
7. b _ o _ h _ r
8. _ n _ l _
9. n _ e _ e / _ e _ h _ w
10. _ r _ n _ f _ t _ e _

Part 2A: Ask a question

Who is she?

✓ **She is my mother. She is not my aunt.**

Who is he?

✓ **He is my uncle. He isn't my father.**

⭐ **Winner's Tip!** Remember: isn't = is not

Part 2B: Fill in the blanks

1. Who is _____?
   She _____ my sister. _____ is not my _____.

2. _____ is he?
   _____ is _____ brother. He is _____ my uncle.

3. _____ is _____?
   She _____ my cousin. She _____ my _____.

4. _____ is _____?
   He is _____ grandfather. He _____ my _____.

Part 3A: Yes / No questions

Is <u>she</u> your <u>grandmother</u>?

✓ **Yes,** she **is.** She **is my** grandmother.
✗ **No,** she **isn't.** She **isn't my** grandmother.

Is <u>he</u> your <u>grandfather</u>?

✓ **Yes,** he **is.** He **is my** grandfather.
✗ **No,** he **isn't.** He **isn't my** grandfather.

Part 3B: Fill in the blanks

1. Is he your _____?
   Yes, he _____. He is my _____.

2. _____ she _____ mother?
   No, _____ isn't. She _____ my _____.

3. _____ he your _____?
   No, he _____. _____ isn't _____ brother.

4. Is _____ _____ niece?
   Yes, _____ is. She _____ _____ niece.

Part 4A: Verb of the day

see / sees – saw – seeing – seen (ver)

Every day, I <u>see</u> my family at breakfast.

On weekends, he <u>sees</u> his uncle at home.

Yesterday, we <u>saw</u> your brother at school.

She is <u>seeing</u> a doctor right now.

I have never <u>seen</u> that action movie.

Part 4B: Verb Practice

1. Every day, I _____ his grandfather.
2. On Tuesdays, she _____ my aunt and her dog.
3. Every Friday, he _____ his friends.
4. Last night, they _____ a TV show.
5. Last week, I _____ his brother at school.
6. Yesterday, you _____ my uncle at the store.
7. Right now, he is _____ a movie.
8. They are _____ a doctor right now.
9. I have never _____ his family before.
10. We have _____ that show many times.

Part 5A: Phonics Practice

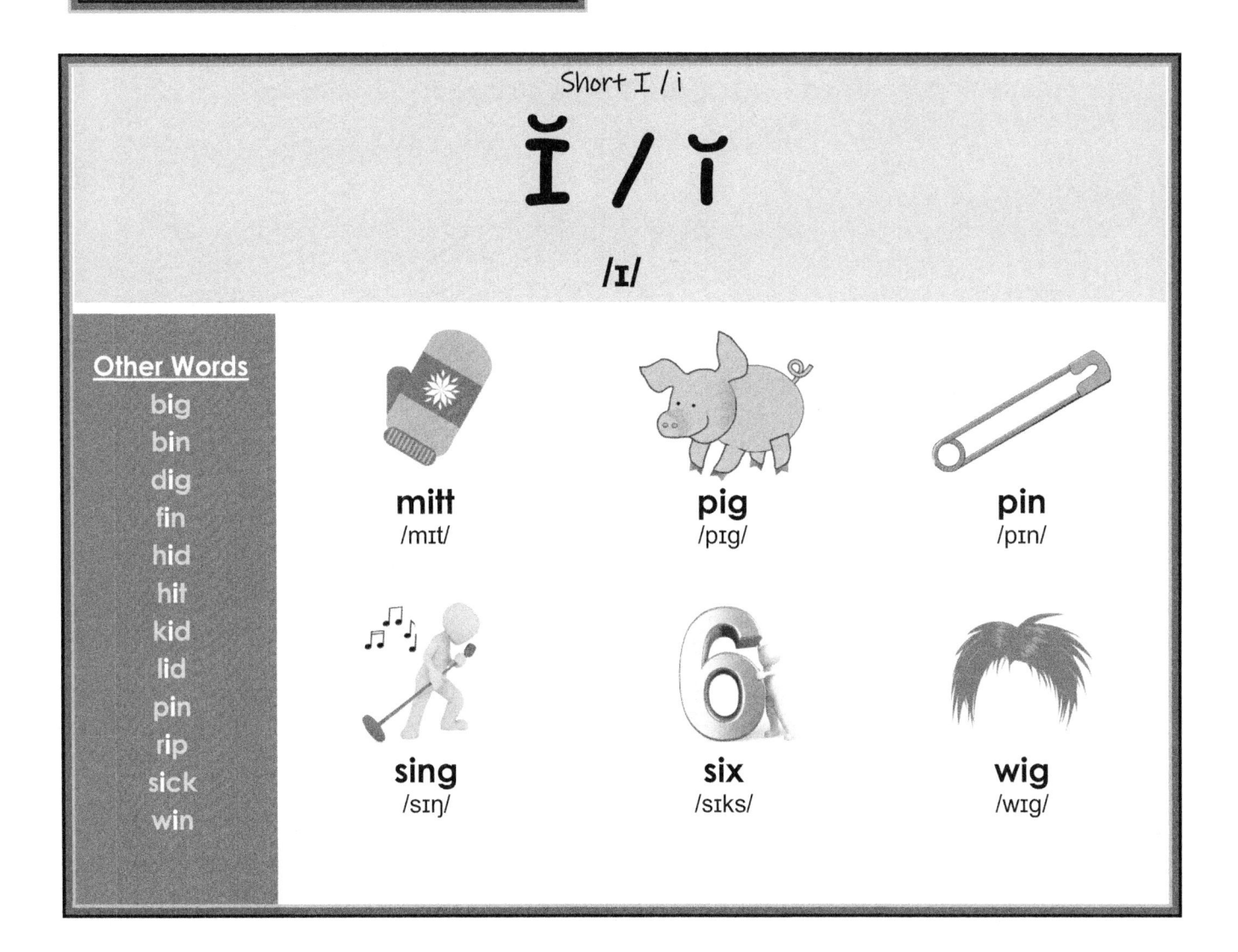

Short I / i

Ĭ / ĭ

/ɪ/

Other Words
big
bin
dig
fin
hid
hit
kid
lid
pin
rip
sick
win

mitt /mɪt/

pig /pɪg/

pin /pɪn/

sing /sɪŋ/

six /sɪks/

wig /wɪg/

Part 5B: Write and read

1. S__x b__g p__gs in w__gs s__ng h__ts.
2. S__ck k__d h__d m__tt r__ps.
3. Jill w__ns p__ns in d__gging b__n l__ds.

Part 6: Fun review

Unscramble the words and write the answers

1. einec _niece_
2. istrse _____
3. lucne _____
4. usconi _____
5. ednorhatmgr _____
6. tmheor _____
7. tanu _____
8. weepnh _____
9. hfraet _____
10. rebotrh _____
11. frdarhanteg _____

Lesson 4: Shapes

formas

Part 1A: Learn the words

1. **circle**
   círculo
2. **oval**
   oval
3. **triangle**
   triângulo
4. **square**
   quadrado
5. **pentagon**
   pentágono
6. **star**
   estrela
7. **rectangle**
   retângulo
8. **octagon**
   octógono
9. **diamond**
   losango
10. **heart**
    coração

⭐ Practice speaking: "*Quadrado*" is "*square*" in English! ⭐

Part 1B: Write the words

Write the missing letters!   Write x 1   Write x 2

1. c _ r _ l _
2. _ v _ l
3. t _ i _ n _ l _
4. _ q _ a _ e
5. p _ n _ a _ o _
6. _ t _ r
7. r _ c _ a _ g _ e
8. _ c _ a _ o _
9. d _ a _ o _ d
10. _ e _ r _

Part 2A: Ask a question

How many squares are there?

✓ **There is one square.**

How many circles are there?

✓ **There are four circles. There aren't five circles.**

⭐ **Winner's Tip!** Remember: aren't = are not

Part 2B: Fill in the blanks

1. How _____ ovals are _____?
   There _____ six _____.

2. _____ many _____ are _____?
   _____ are _____ hearts.

3. _____ _____ _____ are _____?
   _____ is _____ _____.

4. _____ _____ triangles _____ _____?
   There _____ _____ _____.

Part 3A: Yes / No questions

Is there one <u>star</u>?

✓ **Yes, there is. There's one** star.
✗ **No, there is not. There isn't one** star.

Are there <u>seven</u> <u>hearts</u>?

✓ **Yes, there are. There are seven** hearts.
✗ **No, there aren't. There aren't seven** hearts.

⭐ **Winner's Tip!** there's = there is

Part 3B: Fill in the blanks

1. Are there _____ _____?
   Yes, there _____. There _____ two octagons.

2. _____ there one _____?
   No, _____ isn't. There _____ _____ star.

3. _____ there _____ _____?
   No, _____ _____. There aren't four rectangles.

4. Are _____ _____ _____?
   Yes, _____ are. There are _____ pentagons.

Part 4A: Verb of the day

find / finds – found – finding – found (encontrar)

Every evening, we <u>find</u> stars in the sky.

Sometimes, she <u>finds</u> circles on her desk.

Yesterday, we <u>found</u> a blue diamond.

She is <u>finding</u> a triangle right now.

I have never <u>found</u> an octagon.

Part 4B: Verb Practice

1. Every day, we _____ shapes around the room.
2. On many days, he _____ circles on the floor.
3. Every night, she _____ bright stars.
4. Last class, we _____ a pentagon in a picture.
5. Last weekend, I _____ an octagon-shaped room.
6. This morning, they _____ a heart someone drew.
7. Right now, she is _____ triangle-shaped food.
8. I'm _____ a pencil to draw a big rectangle.
9. He has never _____ an oval-shaped eraser.
10. She has _____ many diamonds in the game.

Part 5A: Phonics Practice

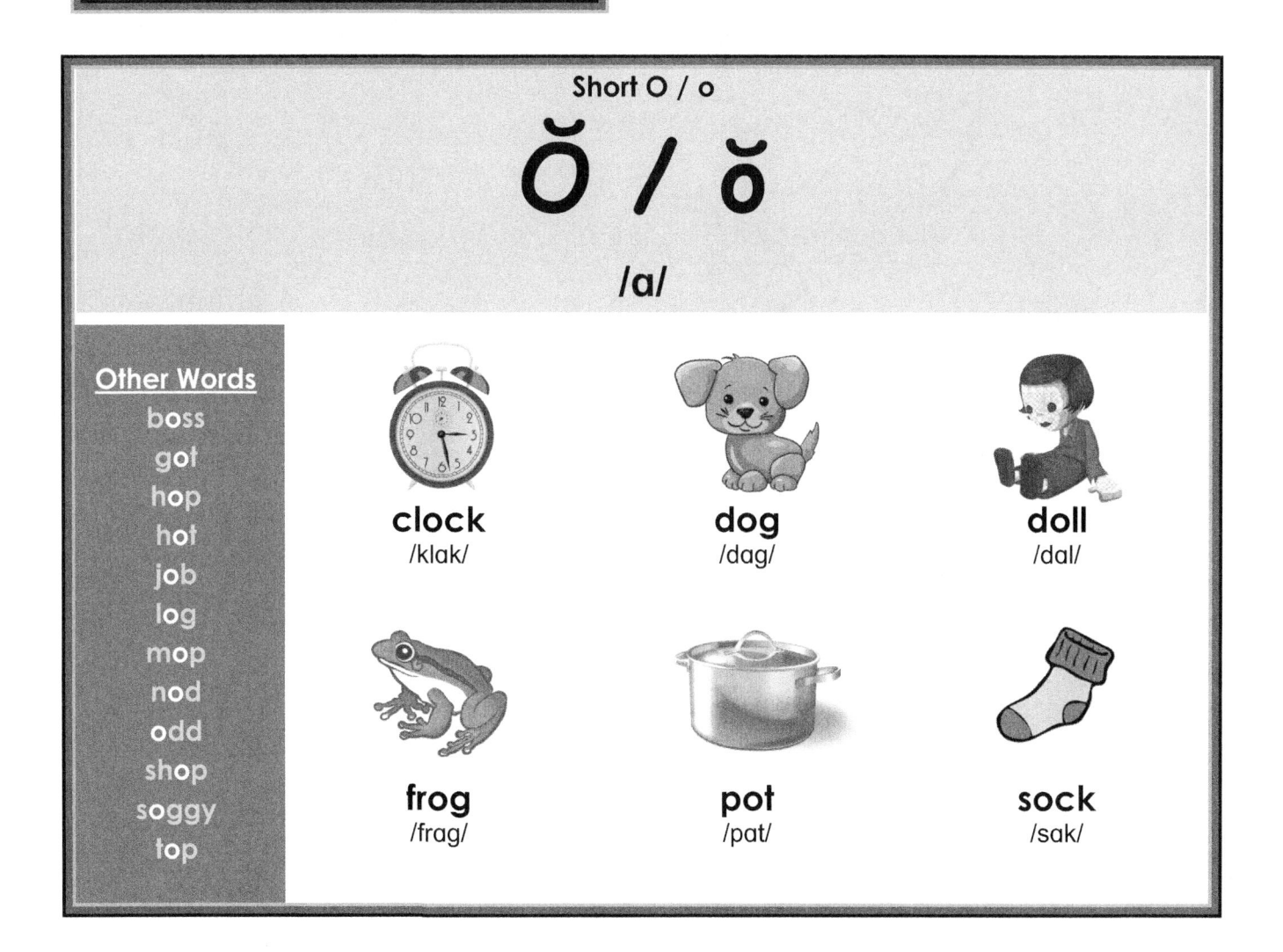

Short O / o

Ŏ / ŏ

/a/

Other Words
boss
got
hop
hot
job
log
mop
nod
odd
shop
soggy
top

clock
/klak/

dog
/dag/

doll
/dal/

frog
/frag/

pot
/pat/

sock
/sak/

Part 5B: Write and read

1. S__ggy fr__gs h__p on h__t p__t t__ps.

2. B__ss d__lls g__t n__dding d__gs __dd j__bs.

3. Tom m__pped Jon's sh__p with s__cks.

Part 6: Fun review

Write the answers

1. How many __squares__ are there?
   There are three squares. There aren't two squares.

2. How many _____ are there?
   _____

3. How many _____ are there?
   _____

4. How many _____ are there?
   _____

Write the questions

1. _Are there six stars?_____
   Yes, there are. There are six __stars__.

2. _____
   No, there aren't. There aren't two _____.

3. _____
   Yes, there are. There are four _____.

4. _____
   Yes, there are. There are five _____.

The two other shapes are _____ and _____.

Lesson 5: At the toy store

na loja de brinquedos

Part 1A: Learn the words

1. **an airplane**
   avião de brinquedo
2. **a ball**
   bola
3. **some blocks**
   blocos
4. **a board game**
   jogo de tabuleiro
5. **a car**
   carro de brinquedos
6. **a dinosaur**
   dinossauro
7. **a doll**
   boneca
8. **a jump rope**
   pular corda
9. **a robot**
   robô
10. **a teddy bear**
    ursinho de pelúcia

⭐ Practice speaking: "_Boneca_" is "_doll_" in English! ⭐

Part 1B: Write the words

Write the missing letters!   Write x 1   Write x 2

1. a__r_l_n__
2. __a__l
3. b__o__k__
4. __o_r_ g__m__
5. __a__
6. d__n_s__u__
7. __o__l
8. j__m__ r_p__
9. __o__o__
10. t__d_y __e__r

25

Part 2A: Ask a question

What do you have?

✓ **I have a doll. I don't have a teddy bear.**

What does he have?

✓ **He has a board game. He doesn't have a car.**

⭐ **Winner's Tip!** he / she / it answer with "has"

Part 2B: Fill in the blanks

1. What _____ she _____?
   _____ has _____. She _____ have a car.

2. _____ do _____ have?
   We _____ _____. We _____ have a ball.

3. What _____ _____ _____?
   They _____ some blocks. They don't have _____.

4. _____ _____ _____ _____?
   He _____ a dinosaur. He doesn't _____ _____.

Part 3A: Yes / No questions

Do you have a dinosaur?

✓ **Yes, I do. I have** a dinosaur.
✗ **No, I do not. I don't have** a dinosaur.

Does she have an airplane?

✓ **Yes, she does. She has** an airplane.
✗ **No, she does not. She doesn't have** an airplane.

⭐ **Winner's Tip!** don't = do not / doesn't = does not

Part 3B: Fill in the blanks

1. _____ you _____ some blocks?
   Yes, I do. _____ _____ _____.

2. _____ she _____ a teddy bear?
   No, _____ _____. She _____ a jump rope.

3. _____ they _____ a car?
   No, _____ _____. _____ don't have a car.

4. Does _____ have _____?
   Yes, _____ does. He _____ _____.

Part 4A: Verb of the day

borrow / borrows – borrowed – borrowing – borrowed (pegar emprestado)

Every week, I <u>borrow</u> a car from him.

Sometimes, she <u>borrows</u> his dinosaur toy.

Yesterday, I <u>borrowed</u> his airplane.

He is <u>borrowing</u> a robot right now.

She has never <u>borrowed</u> anything.

Part 4B: Verb Practice

1. Every Monday, I _____ my friend's blocks.
2. On Tuesdays, he _____ board games from me.
3. Every day, she _____ my jump rope.
4. Last time, we _____ his toy dinosaur.
5. Last week, they _____ some dolls to play with.
6. Yesterday, he _____ my favorite robot.
7. Right now, she is _____ a ball to play a game.
8. They are _____ a car for their vacation.
9. He has never _____ an airplane before.
10. You have _____ my teddy bear many times.

Part 5A: Phonics Practice

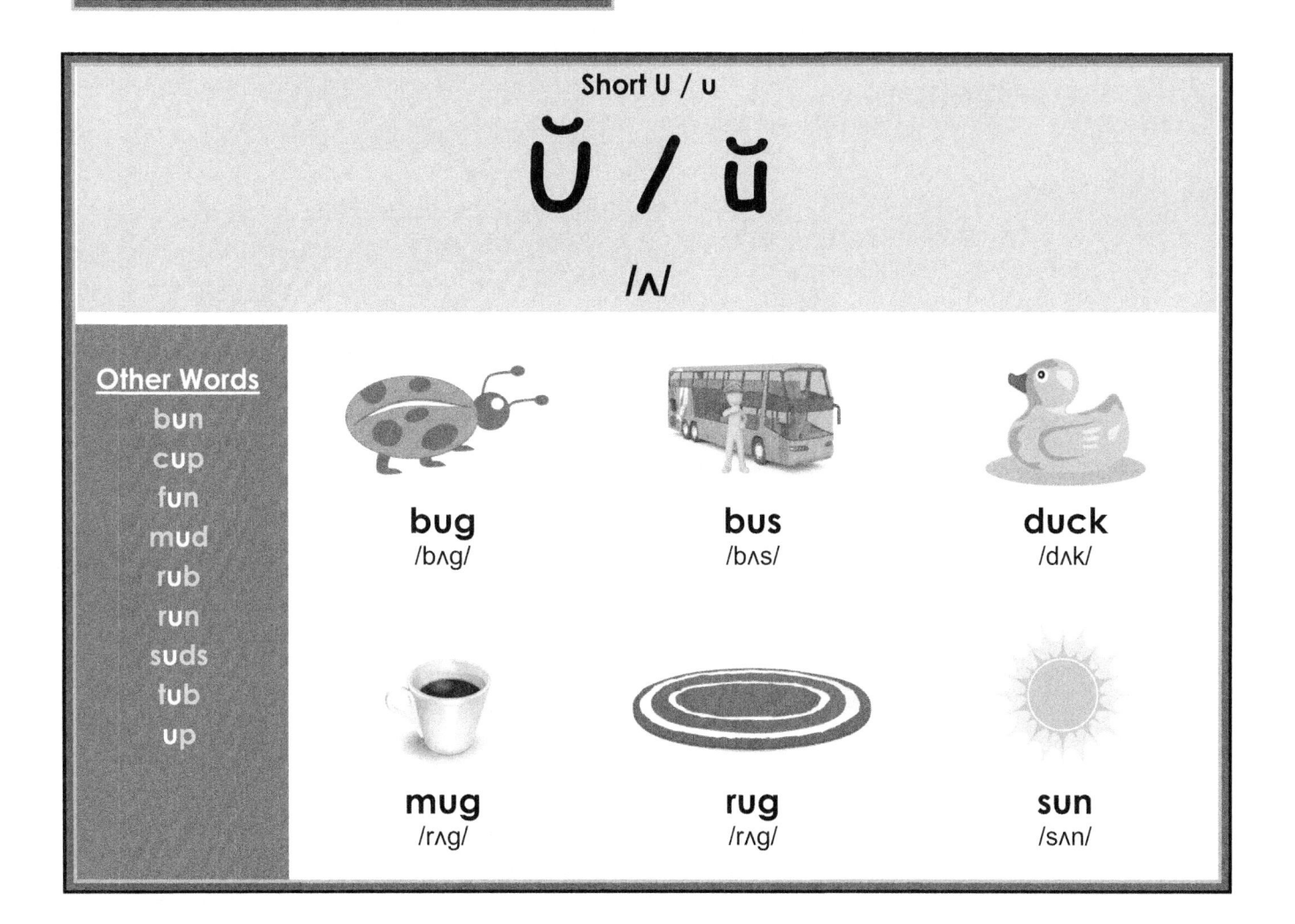

Short U / u

Ŭ / ŭ

/ʌ/

Other Words
bun
cup
fun
mud
rub
run
suds
tub
up

bug
/bʌg/

bus
/bʌs/

duck
/dʌk/

mug
/rʌg/

rug
/rʌg/

sun
/sʌn/

Part 5B: Write and read

1. One f__n b__g r__ns on some r__gs.
2. F__n t__b d__cks r__b s__ds on m__d.
3. A m__g, b__n, and b__s __nder the s__n.

Part 6: Fun review

Write the sentences

1. ✓ car
   ✗ board game

   1. He <u>has a car.</u>
      <u>He doesn't have a board game.</u>

2. ✓ ball
   ✗ airplane

   2. We _____

3. ✓ teddy bear
   ✗ blocks

   3. She _____

Yes or no?

1. ✓ Do you have a dinosaur?
   <u>Yes, I do. I have a dinosaur.</u>

2. ✗ Does she have a robot?

3. ✓ Does he have a jump rope?

TEST 1: Lessons 1 - 5

Write the correct answer next to the letter "A"

A: ___ 1. Is that a _____? Yes, it is. _____ is a marker.
a) marker / That's
b) markers / That
c) marker / That
d) marker / It's

A: ___ 2. What are _____? Those are books. They _____ posters.
a) those / aren't
b) those / are
c) these / don't
d) books / 're not

A: ___ 3. How many _____ _____ there? There is one triangle.
a) triangle / is
b) triangles / are
c) triangles / find
d) triangles / does

A: ___ 4. Who is he? He is my _____. He _____ my uncle.
a) brother / isn't
b) father / 's
c) uncle / been
d) brother / looks

A: ___ 5. What is this? _____ is a pen. It is not a _____.
a) This / eraser
b) It / pen
c) That / ruler
d) This / pencil

A: ___ 6. What do you _____? I have a star. I _____ have a circle.
a) has / don't
b) have / doesn't
c) have / don't
d) had / can't

A: ___ 7. _____ those clocks? Yes, _____ are. Those are clocks.
a) Are / these
b) Is / it
c) Do / those
d) Are / they

A: ___ 8. Is that some _____? No, it _____. That isn't some whiteout.
a) glue / can't
b) whiteout / isn't
c) tape / doesn't
d) whiteout / doesn't

A: ___ 9. Do you _____ a doll? Yes, I _____. I have a doll.
a) have / have
b) has / has
c) has / have
d) have / do

A: ___ **10.** Is she your _____? No, she isn't. She isn't my _____.
a) cousin / cousin **b)** father / father
c) sister / family **d)** nephew / nephew

A: ___ **11.** Right now, she is _____ her keys.
a) find **b)** finds
c) finding **d)** found

A: ___ **12.** What does he _____? He has a car. He doesn't _____ a ball.
a) has / has **b)** have / hold
c) have / have **d)** having / have

A: ___ **13.** Yesterday, we _____ your brother at school.
a) sees **b)** saw
c) see **d)** seen

A: ___ **14.** _____ she have a dinosaur? No, she _____. She doesn't have a dinosaur.
a) Do / don't **b)** Has / hasn't
c) Doesn't / does **d)** Does / doesn't

A: ___ **15.** What are _____? Those are _____. They aren't chairs.
a) these / bookshelves **b)** those / desk
c) those / desks **d)** this / globes

A: ___ **16.** Are there seven _____? Yes, there are. There are seven _____.
a) ovals / ovals **b)** oval / ovals
c) ovals / oval **d)** oval / shapes

A: ___ **17.** Every week, she _____ new pencils and erasers.
a) buy **b)** buys
c) buyed **d)** buying

A: ___ **18.** Sometimes, I _____ money from my aunt.
a) borrowing **b)** borrows
c) have borrow **d)** borrow

Answers on page 129

Lesson 6: Food & drinks

alimentos e bebidas

Part 1A: Learn the words

1. **cake**
   bolo
2. **cheese**
   queijo
3. **coffee**
   café
4. **juice**
   suco
5. **milk**
   leite
6. **pie**
   torta
7. **pizza**
   pizza
8. **soda**
   refrigerante
9. **tea**
   chá
10. **water**
    agua

⭐ Practice speaking: "_Bolo_" is "_cake_" in English! ⭐

Part 1B: Write the words

Write the missing letters!   Write x 1   Write x 2

1. c__k__
2. __h__e__e
3. c__f__e__
4. __u__c__
5. m__l__
6. __i__
7. p__z__a
8. __o__a
9. __e__
10. w__t__r

Part 2A: Ask a question

What do you want?

✓ **I want some cake. I don't want any pie.**

What does he want?

✓ **He wants some tea. He doesn't want any soda.**

⭐ **Winner's Tip!** + some / - any

Part 2B: Fill in the blanks

1. What _____ you _____?
   We _____ some _____. We don't want any pie.

2. _____ does _____ _____?
   He _____ some tea. He _____ want any soda.

3. _____ _____ she _____?
   She _____ _____ pie. She doesn't want any cake.

4. _____ _____ _____ _____?
   They _____ _____ _____. They _____ want any _____.

Part 3A: Yes / No questions

Do <u>you</u> want some <u>water</u>?

✓ **Yes, I do. I want some** water.
✗ **No, I do not. I don't want any** water.

Does <u>she</u> want some <u>juice</u>?

✓ **Yes,** she **does.** She **wants some** juice.
✗ **No,** she **does not.** She **doesn't want any** juice.

⭐ **Winner's Tip!** don't = do not / doesn't = does not

Part 3B: Fill in the blanks

1. Does he _____ some _____?
   Yes, he _____. He _____ _____ juice.

2. Do _____ want _____ _____?
   No, I do not. I _____ want _____ soda.

3. _____ she _____ _____ _____?
   Yes, she _____. She _____ _____ milk.

4. Do _____ _____ _____ tea?
   No, we don't. We _____ _____ _____ tea.

Part 4A: Verb of the day

want / wants – wanted – wanting – wanted (querer)

Sometimes, I <u>want</u> some milk and pie.

Every morning, he <u>wants</u> some coffee.

Last night, we <u>wanted</u> some pizza to eat.

(He is <u>wanting</u> to ask you for some cake.)*

I have never <u>wanted</u> to drink soda.

*less common, polite form

Part 4B: Verb Practice

1. Every breakfast, I _____ a cup of coffee.
2. On Fridays, she _____ pizza for dinner.
3. Every evening, he _____ some soda to drink.
4. Last time, they _____ some juice and soda.
5. Last weekend, I _____ to eat some cake.
6. This morning, we _____ some tea at breakfast.
7. Last night, he _____ to drink some milk.
8. Right now, he is _____ to ask for a drink.*
9. She has never _____ any water with her food.
10. You have _____ some pie for a long time.

Part 5A: Phonics Practice

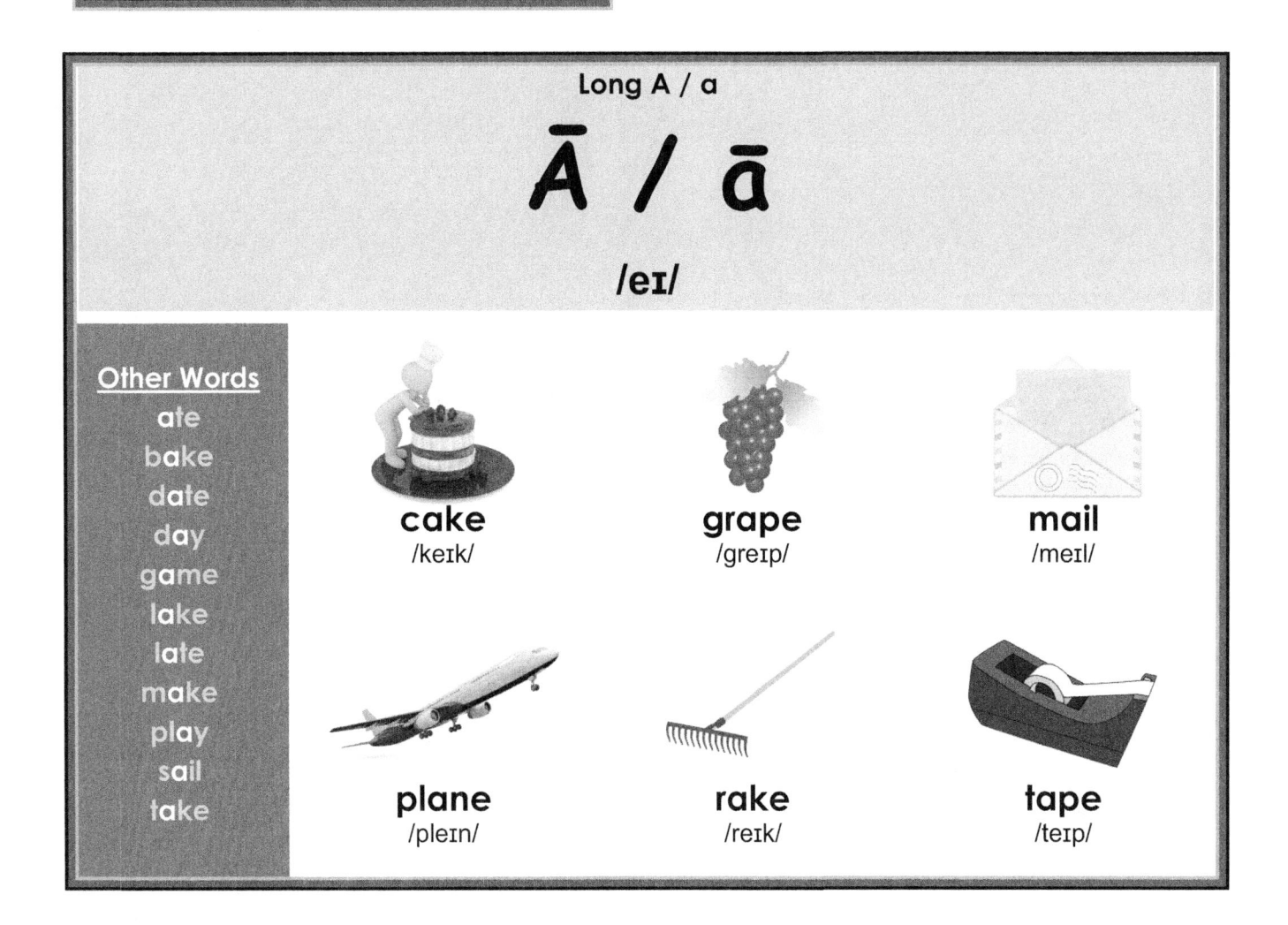

Long A / a

Ā / ā

/eɪ/

Other Words
ate
bake
date
day
game
lake
late
make
play
sail
take

cake
/keɪk/

grape
/greɪp/

mail
/meɪl/

plane
/pleɪn/

rake
/reɪk/

tape
/teɪp/

Part 5B: Write and read

1. May __te gr__pe c__ke by the l__ke.

2. Dale t__kes t__ped r__kes on pl__nes.

3. Jay pl__ys g__mes and m__kes m__il l__te.

Part 6: Fun review

Match the sentences and pictures

What does she want?

Do you want some cake?

What does he want?

Does she want some pie?

What do they want?

Does he want some cheese?

Do they want some pizza?

What do you want?

I don't want any soda.

Yes, they do.

She wants some tea.

No, he doesn't.

Yes, I do.

He wants some water.

No, she doesn't.

They don't want any coffee.

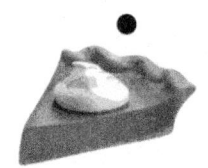

Lesson 7: Vegetables

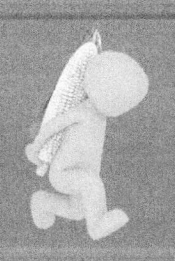

legumes

Part 1A: Learn the words

1. **asparagus**
   espargos
2. **broccoli**
   brócolis
3. **cabbage**
   repolho
4. **carrot**
   cenoura
5. **corn**
   milho
6. **mushroom**
   cogumelo
7. **onion**
   cebola
8. **potato**
   batata
9. **pumpkin**
   abóbora
10. **spinach**
    espinafre

⭐ Practice speaking: "_Milho_" is "_corn_" in English! ⭐

Part 1B: Write the words

Write the missing letters!   Write x 1   Write x 2

1. a_ p_ r_ g_ s
2. _ r_ c_ o_ i
3. c_ b_ a_ e
4. _ a_ r_ t
5. c_ r_
6. _ u_ h_ o_ m
7. o_ i_ n
8. _ o_ a_ o
9. p_ m_ k_ n
10. _ p_ n_ c_

39

Part 2A: Ask a question

What do <u>you</u> want to eat?

✓ **I want to eat some <u>broccoli</u>.**
✗ **I don't want to eat any <u>onion</u>.**

What does <u>she</u> want to eat?

✓ **She wants to eat some <u>carrot</u>.**
✗ **She doesn't want to eat any <u>potato</u>.**

★ **Winner's Tip!** he / she / it verb+ "**s**"

Part 2B: Fill in the blanks

1. What _____ you _____ to eat?
   I _____ to eat some _____.

2. _____ _____ he want _____ eat?
   He _____ to eat _____ _____.

3. _____ does _____ _____ to _____?
   She _____ want _____ eat any _____.

4. What _____ they _____ _____ _____?
   They don't _____ _____ _____ any _____.

Part 3A: Yes / No questions

Do you want to eat some cabbage?

✓ **Yes, I do. I want to eat some** cabbage.
✗ **No, I don't. I don't want to eat any** cabbage.

Does he want to eat some corn?

✓ **Yes, he does. He wants to eat some** corn.
✗ **No, he doesn't. He doesn't want to eat any** corn.

⭐ **Winner's Tip!** Remember: + some / - any

Part 3B: Fill in the blanks

1. Do you _____ to _____ some _____?
   Yes, I do. I _____ to eat _____ mushroom.

2. _____ he _____ to eat some _____?
   No, he _____. He _____ want to eat any corn.

3. _____ they want to _____ _____ pumpkin?
   No, they _____. They don't want to eat any _____.

4. Does _____ want to eat some _____?
   Yes, he _____. He _____ to eat _____ onion.

Part 4A: Verb of the day

cook / cooks – cooked – cooking – cooked (cozinhar)

Every afternoon, I <u>cook</u> some broccoli.

Often, he <u>cooks</u> onion for his breakfast.

Yesterday, we <u>cooked</u> a lot of corn.

She is <u>cooking</u> some pumpkin for dinner.

We have never <u>cooked</u> any asparagus.

Part 4B: Verb Practice

1. Every day, I _____ vegetables for my lunch.
2. On Mondays, he _____ asparagus for his meals.
3. Every Saturday, he _____ corn with his friends.
4. Last night, we _____ some broccoli and potato.
5. Last weekend, I _____ some spinach and onion.
6. Yesterday, he _____ a big meal for everyone.
7. Right now, he is _____ a really big pumpkin.
8. They are _____ many carrots right now.
9. He has never _____ cabbage well before.
10. I have _____ mushroom many times before now.

Part 5A: Phonics Practice

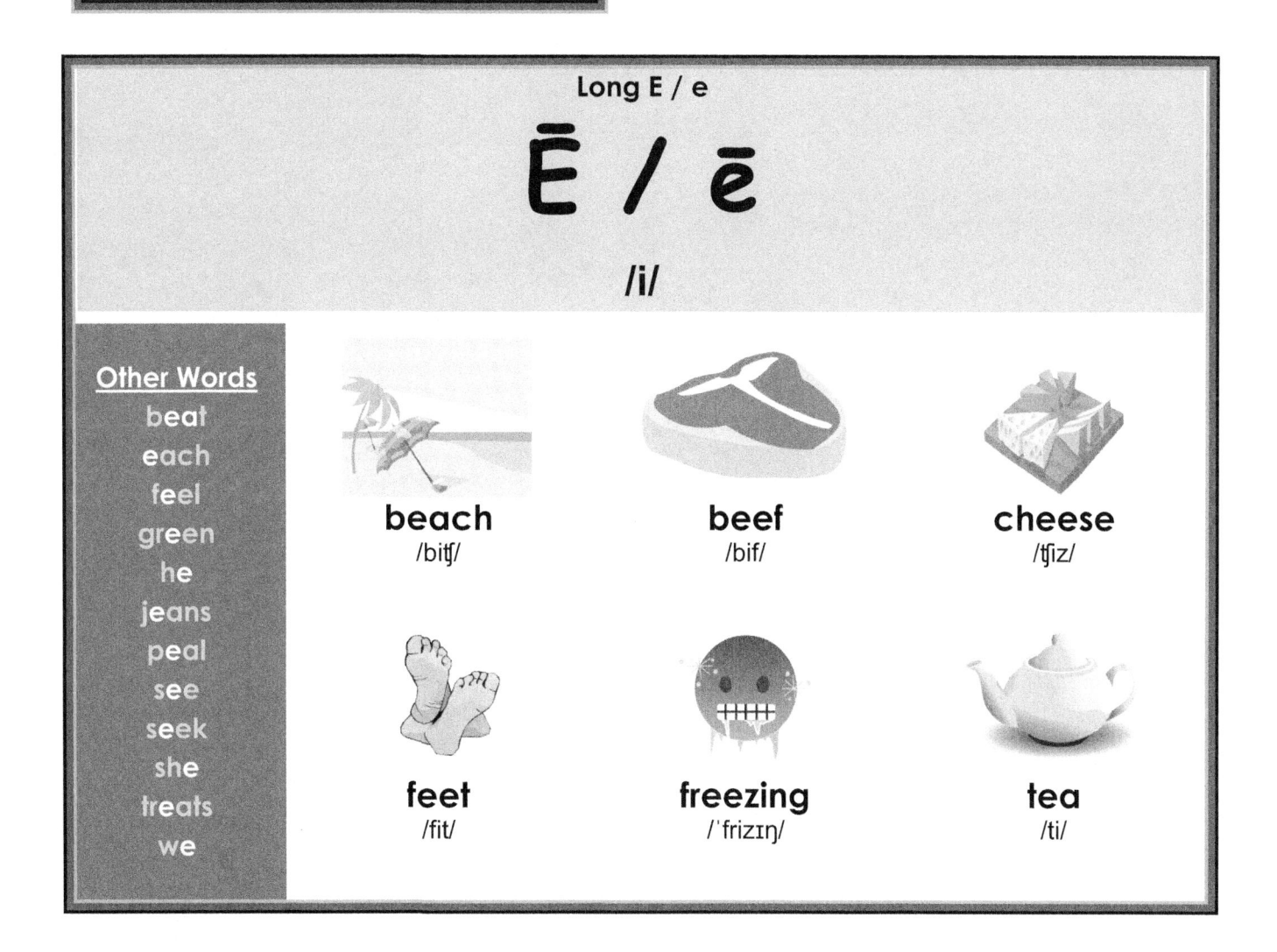

Long E / e
Ē / ē
/i/

Other Words
beat
each
feel
green
he
jeans
peal
see
seek
she
treats
we

beach
/bitʃ/

beef
/bif/

cheese
/tʃiz/

feet
/fit/

freezing
/ˈfrizɪŋ/

tea
/ti/

Part 5B: Write and read

1. M__an Pete __ats b__ef ch__ese tr__ats.
2. W__ s__e gr__en t__a tr__es s__ek s__as.
3. H__ b__ats fr__ezing f__et at __ach b__ach.

Part 6: Fun review

Unscramble the words and find them

smmuoroh
mushroom

nmpkpui
_____

ottpoa
_____

coiocrbl
_____

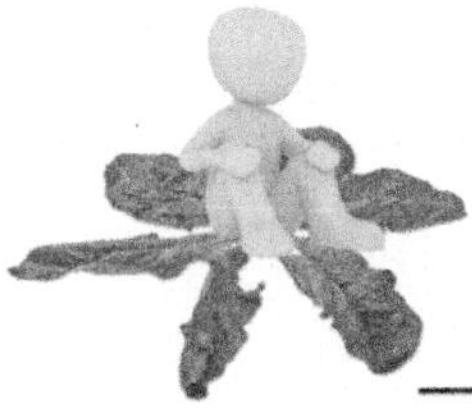

bgabcae
_____

inpcsah
_____

sarsupaga
_____

nooin
_____

rnoc
_____

rctora
_____

```
z z d h q o z f m g e c g x j x g s
m i c p b c e g x r a l c n f j u z
y h n w s h z p o t r o i c j g z o
x h i c b x l o q r k r x d a y t w
x b e v e g e t a b l e s r o h p m
o r c w l x n a k a w q a a c t n s
f o a w d b o t q t r p d a r q s p
b c b j c e k o j f s g n x v q j o
t c b y f u f b c a h i x z z q y o
d o a n p v d z p c p s y a i i o n
x l g w i n n e r s e n g l i s h v
c i e y n g a g o q o f w k r b w z
t a u o p d m g n e m v o l j d t g
x a j o t u v s i m u s h r o o m f
c a r r o t h n o j y s z o k g x i
o v p u m p k i n k a v f z v a q b
r d i f a c h e f s h a t c p g m e
n a u q o h m t j a t t c k p s f x
```

Lesson 8: Colors

as cores

Part 1A: Learn the words

1. **pink**
   rosa
2. **red**
   vermelho
3. **orange**
   laranja
4. **yellow**
   amarelo
5. **green**
   verde
6. **blue**
   azul
7. **purple**
   roxo
8. **white**
   branco
9. **brown**
   castanho
10. **black**
    preto

⭐ Practice speaking: "_Vermelho_" is "_red_" in English! ⭐

Part 1B: Write the words

Write the missing letters!   Write x 1   Write x 2

1. p__n__
2. __e__
3. o__a__g__
4. __e_l_w
5. g_e_n
6. __l_e
7. p_r_l__
8. __h_t__
9. b__o__n
10. __l_c__

Part 2A: Ask a question

What color do <u>you</u> like?

✓ I like <u>pink</u>, but I don't like <u>green</u>.

What color does <u>she</u> like?

✓ She likes <u>black</u>, but she doesn't like <u>orange</u>.

⭐ **Winner's Tip!** "but" for contrast

Part 2B: Fill in the blanks

1. What _____ does _____ like?
   He _____ blue, but he _____ like _____.

2. What _____ do _____ like?
   They _____ yellow, but they _____ like _____.

3. _____ color _____ she _____?
   She _____ red, but she _____ _____ _____.

4. _____ color _____ _____ _____?
   I _____ pink, but I _____ _____ _____.

> Part 3A: Yes / No questions

Do you like the color red?

✓ **Yes, I do.** I like the color red.
✗ **No, I don't.** I don't like the color red.

Does he like the color blue?

✓ **Yes, he does. He likes** the color blue.
✗ **No, he doesn't. He doesn't like** the color blue.

⭐ **Winner's Tip!** (the color) = optional

> Part 3B: Fill in the blanks

1. _____ you _____ the color green?
   Yes, I do. I _____ the _____ _____.

2. _____ he _____ the color orange?
   No, he _____. He _____ like _____.

3. Do _____ like _____?
   No, I _____. I _____ _____ purple.

4. Does _____ like _____?
   Yes, she _____. She _____ the color _____.

Part 4A: Verb of the day

draw / draws – drew – drawing – drawn (desenhar)

I <u>draw</u> red apples every art class.

She usually <u>draws</u> with a black pencil.

Yesterday, she <u>drew</u> an orange carrot.

He is <u>drawing</u> a picture right now.

She has never <u>drawn</u> a purple car.

Part 4B: Verb Practice

1. Every evening, we _____ many different shapes.
2. On Fridays, she _____ lots of colorful pictures.
3. Sometimes, he _____ pictures of his family.
4. Yesterday, we _____ green dinosaurs for fun.
5. Last week, she _____ something in red crayon.
6. Earlier today, he _____ some vegetables.
7. Right now, she is _____ with her black pencil.
8. We are _____ in the classroom right now.
9. She has never _____ any food or drinks before.
10. I have _____ so many pictures this week.

Part 5A: Phonics Practice

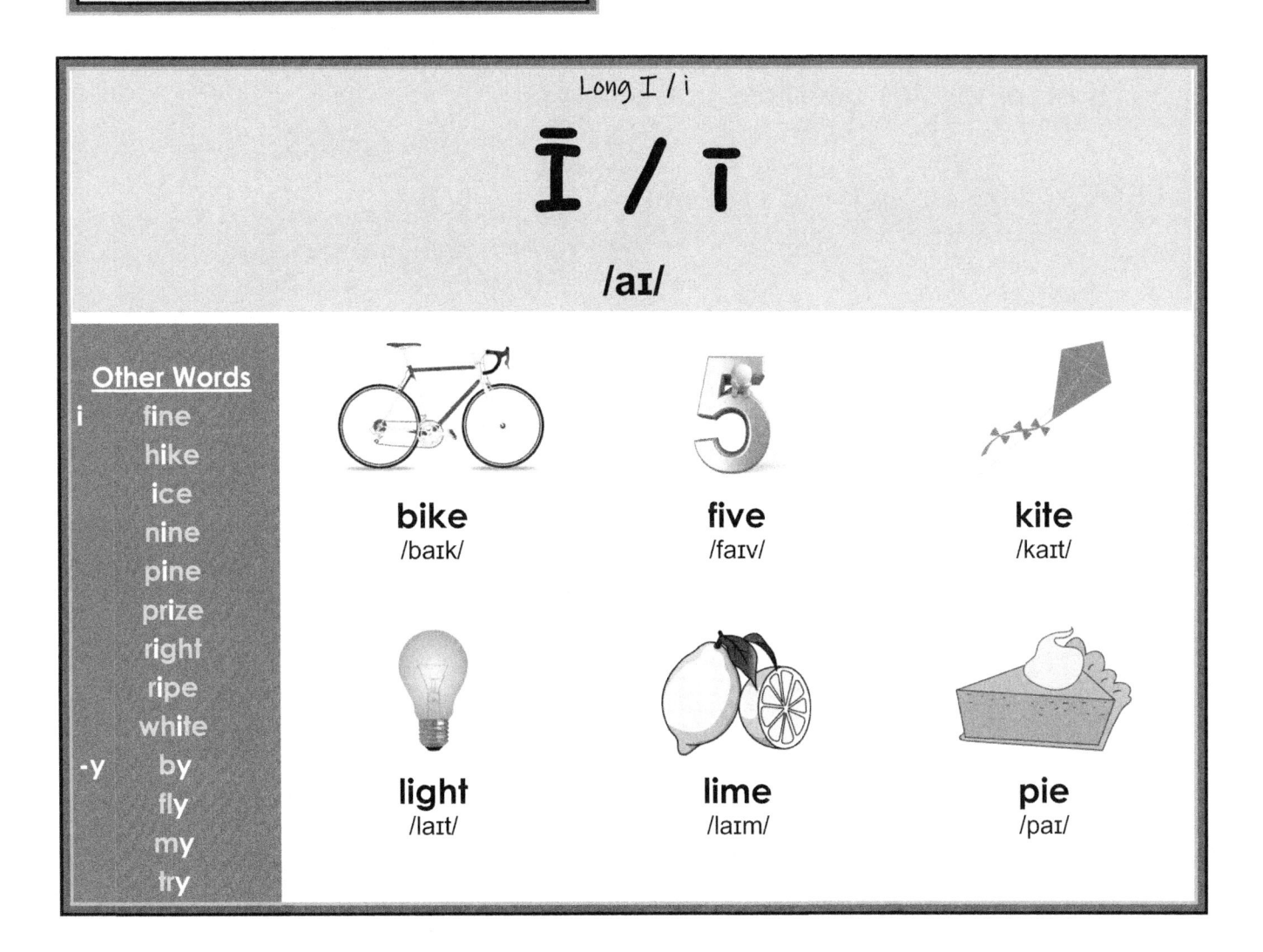

Long I / i
Ī / ī
/aɪ/

Other Words

i: fine, hike, ice, nine, pine, prize, right, ripe, white

-y: by, fly, my, try

bike /baɪk/

five /faɪv/

kite /kaɪt/

light /laɪt/

lime /laɪm/

pie /paɪ/

Part 5B: Write and read

1. Tr__ m__ f__ve pr__zed r__pe l__me p__es.

2. F__nd n__ne r__ght s__zed b__ke l__ghts.

3. H__ke wh__te __ce to fly k__tes b__ p__nes.

Part 6: Fun review

Unscramble the questions and answers

What color does he like?
He doesn't like purple but he likes brown.

_____
_____

_____
_____

_____
_____ ?

_____
_____ ?

Lesson 9: At the fruit market

no mercado de frutas

Part 1A: Learn the words

1. **apple**
   maçã
2. **banana**
   banana
3. **cherry**
   cereja
4. **grape**
   uva
5. **lemon**
   limão
6. **orange**
   laranja
7. **pear**
   pera
8. **pineapple**
   abacaxi
9. **strawberry**
   morango
10. **watermelon**
    melancia

⭐ Practice speaking: "_Maçã_" is "_apple_" in English! ⭐

Part 1B: Write the words

Write the missing letters!   Write x 1   Write x 2

1. __p__l__
2. b__n__n__
3. __h__r__y
4. g__a__e
5. __e__o__
6. o__a__g__
7. __e__r
8. p__n__a__p__e
9. __t__a__b__r__y
10. w__t__r__e__o__

Part 2A: Ask a question

What color is <u>this</u> <u>apple</u>?

✓ **This** apple is <u>green</u>. It isn't <u>red</u>.

What color are <u>these</u> <u>grapes</u>?

✓ **These** grapes are <u>purple</u>. They aren't <u>pink</u>.

⭐ **Winner's Tip!** this, that / these, those

Part 2B: Fill in the blanks

1. _____ color are _____ bananas?
   Those _____ _____ brown. They aren't _____.

2. What _____ _____ these _____?
   _____ cherries are red. They _____ _____.

3. _____ _____ is _____ pineapple?
   This _____ is green. _____ isn't _____.

4. What _____ are _____ _____?
   Those pears _____ pink. _____ _____ _____.

52

Part 3A: Yes / No questions

Is that banana yellow?

✓ **Yes, it is.** That's a yellow banana.
✗ **No, it isn't.** That isn't a yellow banana.

Are these strawberries red?

✓ **Yes, they are.** These are red strawberries.
✗ **No, they aren't.** These aren't red strawberries.

⭐ **Winner's Tip!** Plural: word ending -y becomes -ies

Part 3B: Fill in the blanks

1. Are these _____ orange?
   No, they _____. These _____ _____ lemons.

2. Is _____ watermelon _____?
   No, _____ isn't. This _____ a blue _____.

3. _____ those _____ black?
   No, _____ _____. _____ aren't black grapes.

4. Are _____ _____ _____?
   Yes, _____ are. These _____ _____ lemons.

Part 4A: Verb of the day

need / needs – needed – needing – needed (precisar)

Every day, I <u>need</u> to eat some fruit.

Sometimes, he <u>needs</u> orange juice.

Yesterday, I <u>needed</u> to buy apples.

She is <u>needing</u> more vitamin C.*

Lately, we have <u>needed</u> many things.

*needing = less common

Part 4B: Verb Practice

1. Every day, I _____ to eat more vegetables.
2. On Mondays, he _____ a coffee before work.
3. Every morning, she _____ to buy new pencils.
4. Last time, they _____ to get some strawberries.
5. Last month, I _____ a new chair for my classroom.
6. Yesterday, she _____ to call her brother and sister.
7. Right now, he is _____ some help with school.*
8. They are _____ happier teachers and students.*
9. He has never _____ many toys to have fun.
10. We have _____ some new books for a long time.

Part 5A: Phonics Practice

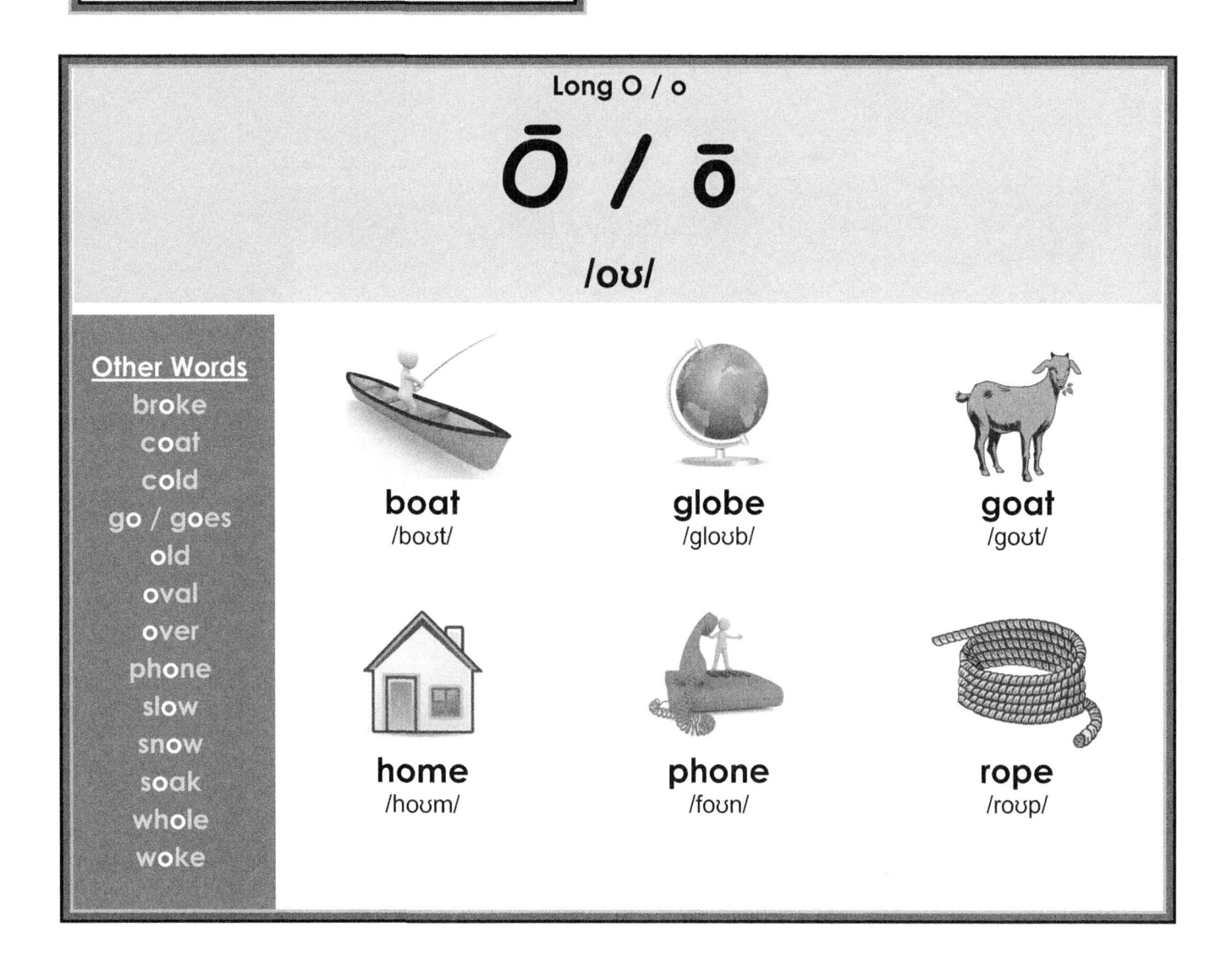

Long O / o

Ō / ō

/oʊ/

Other Words
broke
coat
cold
go / goes
old
oval
over
phone
slow
snow
soak
whole
woke

boat
/boʊt/

globe
/gloʊb/

goat
/goʊt/

home
/hoʊm/

phone
/foʊn/

rope
/roʊp/

Part 5B: Write and read

1. G__at's b__at g__es sl__w __ver the gl__be.

2. S__aked __ld r__pes br__ke c__ld sn__w.

3. The __val ph__ne w__ke the wh__le h__me.

Part 6: Fun review

Unscramble + this / these + match

- What color is __this__ __apple__?
  __This__ __apple__ is pink. [elpap]

- What color are _____ _____?
  _____ _____ are purple. [rpsega]

- What color are _____ _____?
  _____ _____ are red. [aresswerritb]

- What color is _____ _____?
  _____ _____ is brown. [aplipneep]

- What color is _____ _____?
  _____ _____ is yellow. [erap]

- What color is _____ _____?
  _____ _____ is green. [naanba]

Lesson 10: Feelings

sentimentos

Part 1A: Learn the words

1. **angry**
   zangado
2. **bored**
   entediado
3. **fine**
   bem
4. **excited**
   animado
5. **energetic**
   energético
6. **frustrated**
   frustrado
7. **happy**
   feliz
8. **sad**
   triste
9. **sick**
   doente
10. **tired**
    cansado

⭐ Practice speaking: "_Feliz_" is "_happy_" in English! ⭐

Part 1B: Write the words

Write the missing letters!   Write x 1   Write x 2

1. a__g__y
2. __o__e__
3. e__e__g__t__c
4. __x__i__e__
5. f__n__
6. __r__s__r__t__d
7. h__p__y
8. __a__
9. s__c__
10. __i__e__

Part 2A: Ask a question

How are <u>you</u> feeling right now?

✓ **Right now, I'm feeling <u>happy</u>. I'm not feeling <u>sad</u>.**

How is <u>he</u> feeling right now?

✓ **Right now, he's feeling <u>bored</u>. He's not feeling <u>excited</u>.**

⭐ **Winner's Tip!** you're not = you aren't / he's not = he isn't / she's not = she isn't / it's not = it isn't / we're not = we aren't / they're not = they aren't

Part 2B: Fill in the blanks

1. _____ are _____ feeling _____ now?
   Right now, I'm _____ sick. _____ not feeling fine.

2. _____ is _____ _____ right now?
   Right now, he's _____ excited. He's not feeling _____.

3. _____ is _____ _____ _____ now?
   She's feeling _____. She's _____ _____ angry.

4. _____ are _____ _____ _____ now?
   They're _____ tired. They're not _____ _____.

Part 3A: Yes / No questions

Are <u>you</u> feeling <u>angry</u> right now?

✓ **Yes, I am.** I'm feeling angry right now.
✗ **No, I'm not.** I'm not feeling angry right now.

Is <u>she</u> feeling <u>tired</u> right now?

✓ **Yes, she is.** She's feeling tired right now.
✗ **No, she's not.** She isn't feeling tired right now.

⭐ **Winner's Tip!** "right now" = optional

Part 3B: Fill in the blanks

1. Is she _____ energetic _____ now?
   Yes, she is. _____ _____ _____ right now.

2. Are you _____ _____ right _____?
   No, I'm not. _____ not _____ happy right now.

3. _____ they _____ sick _____ _____?
   No, they're not. They're not _____ _____ right now.

4. Is _____ _____ bored _____ _____?
   Yes, he is. He's _____ _____ right now.

Part 4A: Verb of the day

think / thinks – thought – thinking – thought (pensar)

Every day, I <u>think</u> of new ways to be happy.

Sometimes, he <u>thinks</u> angry thoughts.

Yesterday, we <u>thought</u> about what to eat.

She is <u>thinking</u> about her family right now.

I have never <u>thought</u> about his feelings.

Part 4B: Verb Practice

1. Each day, I _____ about what to eat for lunch.
2. On Wednesdays, she _____ of something to cook.
3. Every Tuesday, he _____ about his brother.
4. Yesterday, they _____ about their favorite toys.
5. Last week, we _____ of a way to fix the problem.
6. Earlier today, I _____ about my family.
7. Right now, he is _____ about watching a movie.
8. They are _____ about moving to a new house.
9. He has never _____ about that problem before.
10. You have _____ of many different examples.

Part 5A: Phonics Practice

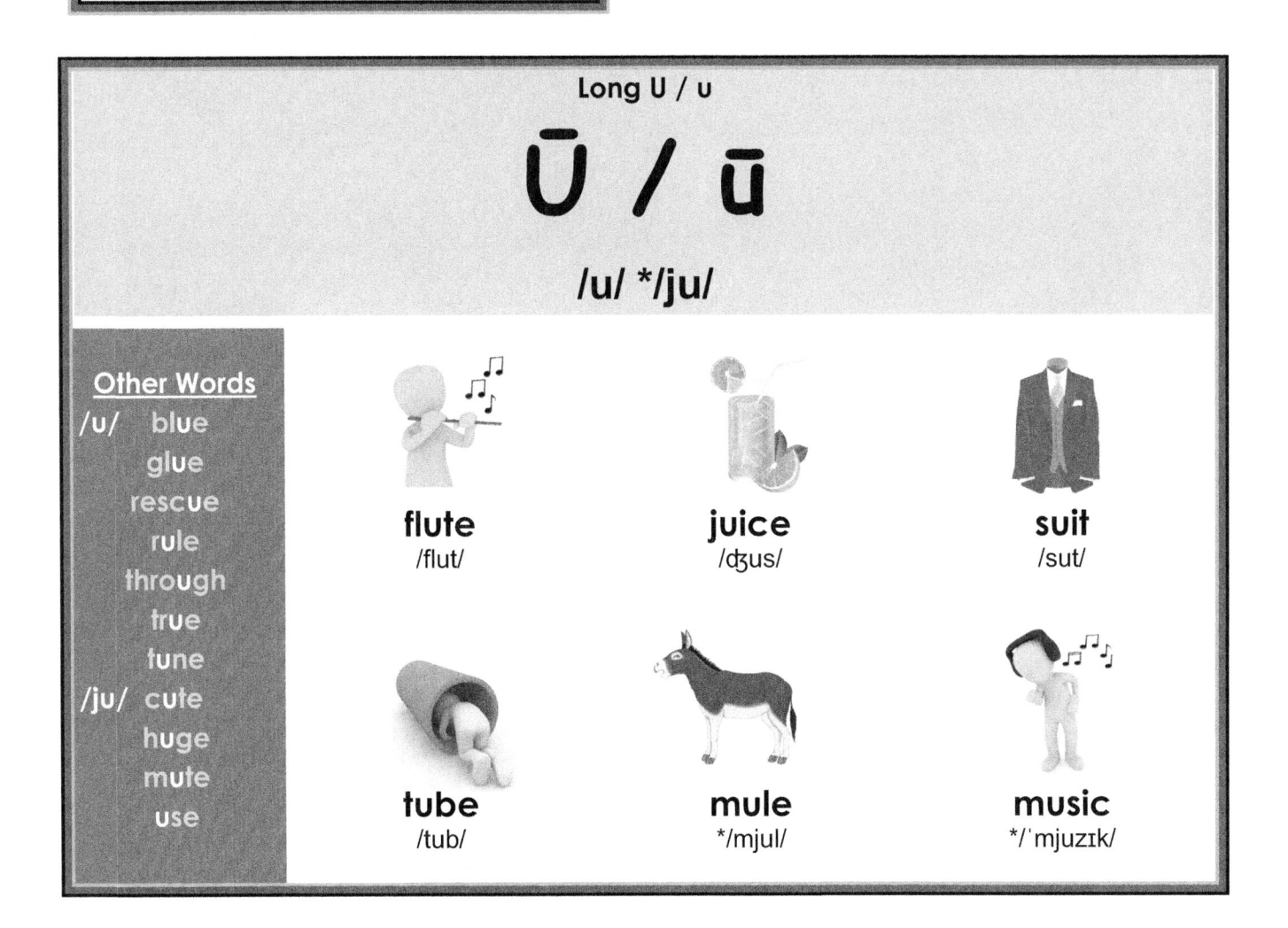

Long U / u

Ū / ū

/u/ */ju/

Other Words
/u/ blue
glue
rescue
rule
through
true
tune
/ju/ cute
huge
mute
use

flute
/flut/

juice
/dʒus/

suit
/sut/

tube
/tub/

mule
*/mjul/

music
*/ˈmjuzɪk/

Part 5B: Write and read

1. Tr__e s__it r__les resc__e bl__e j__ice.

2. Fl__te t__nes blew gl__e thro__gh t__bes.

*3. H__ge c__te m__les __se m__ted m__sic.

Part 6: Fun review

Complete the sentences, write the words

1. Right now, he's feeling s_a_d. He isn't feeling t_____d.

   s____d   t____d   f____e   b____d   e_____c

2. Right now, she's feeling s____k. She's not feeling f_____d.

   h____y   s____k   a____y   e____d   f_____d

3. How are you feeling right now?

   _____

TEST 2: Lessons 6 - 10

Write the correct answer next to the letter "A"

A: ___ 1. What does he _____ to eat? He _____ want to eat any corn.
a) wants / does
b) want / doesn't
c) wanting / don't
d) want / don't

A: ___ 2. What color _____ they like? They like red, but they _____ like blue.
a) does / doesn't
b) do / doesn't
c) are / aren't
d) do / don't

A: ___ 3. What color _____ these pears? These pears _____ red.
a) are / are
b) do / colored
c) is / color
d) are / color is

A: ___ 4. What do you want? I want _____ tea. I don't want _____ coffee.
a) any / some
b) much / lots of
c) some / many
d) some / any

A: ___ 5. Is he _____ sad right now? Yes, he _____. He's feeling sad.
a) feel / does
b) feels / feels
c) feeling / is
d) feeling / feeling

A: ___ 6. _____ this lemon green? Yes, it is. _____ is a green lemon.
a) Does / It
b) Is / This
c) Do / It's
d) Are / These

A: ___ 7. Last night, we _____ many different colors on the paper.
a) draw
b) drawing
c) drew
d) drawn

A: ___ 8. _____ she want some pie? Yes, she does. She _____ some pie.
a) Do / want
b) Would / wanting
c) Does / wants
d) Does / want

A: ___ 9. He is _____ some vegetables for lunch.
a) cooking
b) cook
c) cooked
d) cooks

A: ___ **10.** _____ she like the color yellow? No, she _____. She doesn't like the color yellow.
a) Do / don't **b)** Does / doesn't
c) Does / doesn't like **d)** Does / don't like

A: ___ **11.** Every day after work, he _____ to sleep.
a) want **b)** wanting
c) has want **d)** wants

A: ___ **12.** Last weekend, I _____ to visit my sick friend.
a) need **b)** needing
c) needs **d)** needed

A: ___ **13.** How is she _____ right now? Right now, _____ feeling excited.
a) feel / she is **b)** felt / she
c) feeling / she's **d)** feels / she has

A: ___ **14.** Every month, he _____ about traveling around the world.
a) thinks **b)** think
c) thinking **d)** is thought

A: ___ **15.** Do you ____ the color pink? Yes, I _____. I like the color pink.
a) like / like **b)** liking / does
c) likes / do **d)** like / do

A: ___ **16.** Do _____ want to eat some onion? No, they _____. They don't want to eat any onion.
a) them / aren't **b)** they / don't
c) we / doesn't **d)** they / doesn't

A: ___ **17.** How are _____ feeling right now? Right now, _____ feeling fine.
a) you / I can **b)** we / we'll
c) they / they're **d)** they / they'll

A: ___ **18.** He really _____ _____ red onions for a long time.
a) hasn't / cooked **b)** hasn't / cooking
c) didn't / cooked **d)** doesn't / cooks

Answers on page 129

Lesson 11: At the zoo

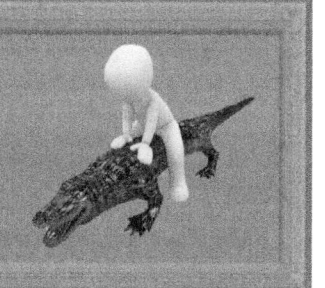

no jardim zoológico

Part 1A: Learn the words

1. **bear**
   urso
2. **crocodile**
   crocodilo
3. **elephant**
   elefante
4. **giraffe**
   girafa
5. **kangaroo**
   canguru
6. **lion**
   leão
7. **monkey**
   macaco
8. **penguin**
   pinguim
9. **rhino**
   rinoceronte
10. **tiger**
    tigre

⭐ Practice speaking: "_Macaco_" is "_monkey_" in English! ⭐

Part 1B: Write the words

Write the missing letters!   Write x 1   Write x 2

1. _ e _ r
2. c _ o _ o _ i _ e
3. _ l _ p _ a _ t
4. g _ r _ f _ e
5. _ a _ g _ r _ o
6. l _ o _
7. _ o _ k _ y
8. p _ n _ u _ n
9. _ h _ n _
10. t _ g _ r

Part 2A: Ask a question

Where is the monkey?

✓ **The monkey is next to the crocodile.**

Where are the elephants?

✓ **The elephants are across from the giraffes.**

⭐ **Winner's Tip!** Learn: next to, across from, between, near

Part 2B: Fill in the blanks

1. where _____ the _____?
   The tigers are _____ the lions and the _____.

2. _____ is _____ kangaroo?
   The _____ is _____ the _____.

3. where _____ _____ _____?
   The giraffe _____ _____ the _____.

4. _____ are _____ _____?
   The rhinos _____ _____ _____ _____.

Part 3A: Yes / No questions

Is the <u>bear</u> <u>between</u> the <u>tiger</u> and the <u>rhino</u>?

✓ **Yes, it is. It's between the** tiger **and the** rhino.
✗ **No, it isn't. It isn't between the** tiger **and the** rhino.

Are the <u>kangaroos</u> <u>near</u> the <u>penguins</u>?

✓ **Yes, they are. They're near the** penguins.
✗ **No, they aren't. They aren't near the** penguins.

★ **Winner's Tip!** remember "s"!

Part 3B: Fill in the blanks

1. Are the crocodiles _____ the bear?
   Yes, they _____. They're across from the _____.

2. _____ the elephant _____ the _____?
   No, it _____. It _____ next to the _____.

3. Is _____ monkey _____ the lion and the _____?
   No, it isn't. It isn't _____ the _____ and the rhino.

4. Are _____ penguins _____ the crocodile?
   Yes, _____ are. _____ near _____ crocodile.

Part 4A: Verb of the day

like / likes – liked – liking – liked (gostar)

Every spring, they <u>like</u> going to the zoo.

He always <u>likes</u> seeing the lions and tigers.

Last time, we <u>liked</u> the giraffes the best.

She is <u>liking</u> her new job at the zoo.

I have never <u>liked</u> crocodiles very much.

Part 4B: Verb Practice

1. Every morning, I _____ eating apples and oranges.
2. On weekends, she _____ spending time with family.
3. Most days, he _____ playing with his many toys.
4. Last week, they _____ the grapes we gave them.
5. Yesterday, I _____ the pencil I saw at the store.
6. This morning, he _____ the color of the sky.
7. Right now, she is _____ the nearby fruit market.
8. They are _____ the food and drinks at the party.
9. He has never _____ the color yellow in his room.
10. We have _____ many kinds of tea before.

Part 5A: Phonics Practice

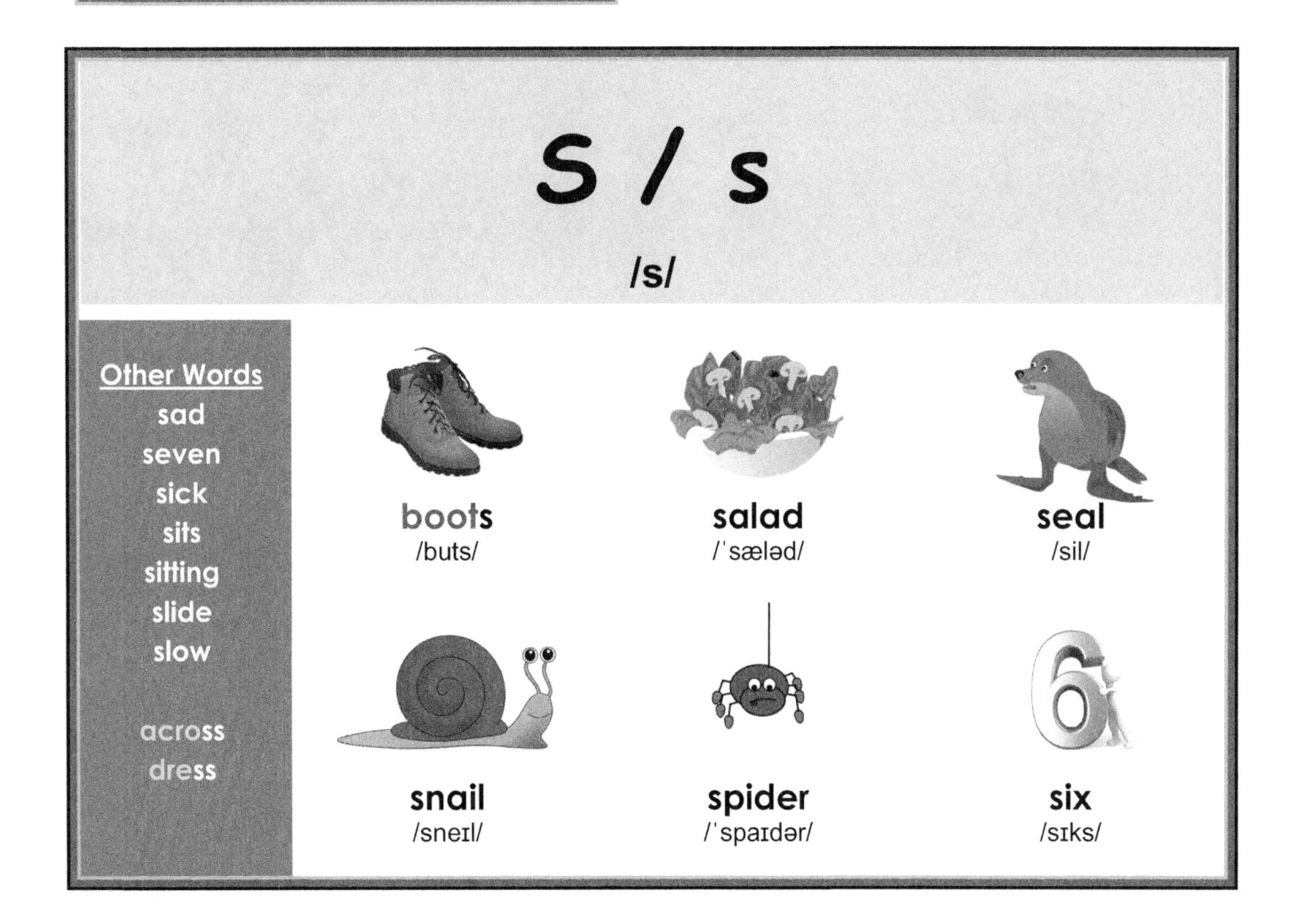

S / s
/s/

Other Words
sad
seven
sick
sits
sitting
slide
slow

across
dress

boots
/buts/

salad
/ˈsæləd/

seal
/sil/

snail
/sneɪl/

spider
/ˈspaɪdər/

six
/sɪks/

Part 5B: Write and read

1. __even __ad __eals mi__s __itting on ice.

2. __ix __low __nails __lide acro__s __alad.

3. A __ick __pider __it__ in boot__ and a dre__s.

Part 6: Fun review

"Is" or "are"? Answer the questions

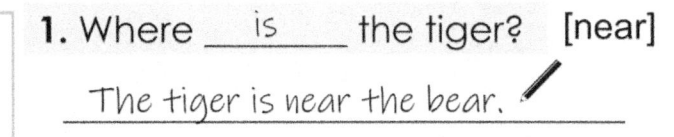

1. Where __is__ the tiger? [near]
   The tiger is near the bear.

2. Where _____ the monkeys? [between]
   _____

3. Where _____ the rhino? [across from]
   _____

4. Where _____ the kangaroos? [between]
   _____

5. Where _____ the penguins? [next to]
   _____

6. Where _____ the bear? [across from]
   _____

70

Lesson 12: Clothes

roupas

Part 1A: Learn the words

1. **blouse**
   blusa
2. **coat**
   casaco
3. **dress**
   vestir
4. **hat**
   chapéu
5. **jacket**
   jaqueta
6. **necktie**
   gravata
7. **scarf**
   cachecol
8. **skirt**
   saia
9. **sweater**
   suéter
10. **T-shirt**
    camiseta

⭐ Practice speaking: "_Cachecol_" is "_scarf_" in English! ⭐

Part 1B: Write the words

Write the missing letters!   Write x 1   Write x 2

1. b__o__s__
2. __o__t
3. d__e__s
4. __a__
5. j__c__e__
6. __e__k__i__
7. s__a__f
8. __k__r__
9. s__e__t__r
10. __-s__i__t

Part 2A: Ask a question

What are you wearing?

✓ I'm wearing a <u>hat</u>. I'm not wearing a <u>scarf</u>.

What is he wearing?

✓ He's wearing a <u>coat</u>. He isn't wearing a <u>T-shirt</u>.

⭐ **Winner's Tip!** I'm = I am / he's = he is / she's = she is / you're = you are / we're = we are / they're = they are

Part 2B: Fill in the blanks

1. What _____ you _____?
   I'm wearing a _____. I'm _____ _____ a hat.

2. _____ is _____ wearing?
   He's _____ a coat. _____ isn't wearing a _____.

3. What _____ _____ _____?
   She's _____ a blouse. She _____ _____ a dress.

4. _____ are _____ _____?
   _____ wearing a _____. I'm not _____ a scarf.

Part 3A: Yes / No questions

Are you wearing a dress?

✓ **Yes, I am. I'm wearing a** dress.
✗ **No, I'm not. I'm not wearing a** dress.

Is she wearing a jacket?

✓ **Yes, she is. She's wearing a** jacket.
✗ **No, she isn't. She isn't wearing a** jacket.

⭐ **Winner's Tip!** remember "a"!

Part 3B: Fill in the blanks

1. Is _____ wearing a _____?
   Yes, he _____. _____ wearing _____ T-shirt.

2. Are _____ _____ a sweater?
   No, _____ not. _____ not _____ a sweater.

3. _____ she _____ a necktie?
   No, _____ _____. _____ isn't wearing a necktie.

4. Are _____ _____ a _____?
   Yes, I _____. _____ wearing _____ jacket.

Part 4A: Verb of the day

wear / wears – wore – wearing – worn (vestir)

On cold days, I <u>wear</u> a very warm jacket.

Sometimes, she <u>wears</u> her new blouse.

Yesterday, they <u>wore</u> green sweaters.

He is <u>wearing</u> a T-shirt and a hat right now.

She has never <u>worn</u> a skirt to school.

Part 4B: Verb Practice

1. Every winter, I _____ my warmest coat and scarf.
2. On Saturdays, she _____ her favorite clothes.
3. Every Sunday, he _____ a jacket for his job.
4. Last month, they _____ yellow scarves at school.
5. Last Monday, I _____ my old ugly jacket outside.
6. Yesterday, she _____ a blue T-shirt and a red skirt.
7. Right now, he is _____ an expensive black sweater.
8. I'm _____ a long gray necktie right now.
9. He has never _____ the coat that I gave to him.
10. You have _____ that purple T-shirt many times.

Part 5A: Phonics Practice

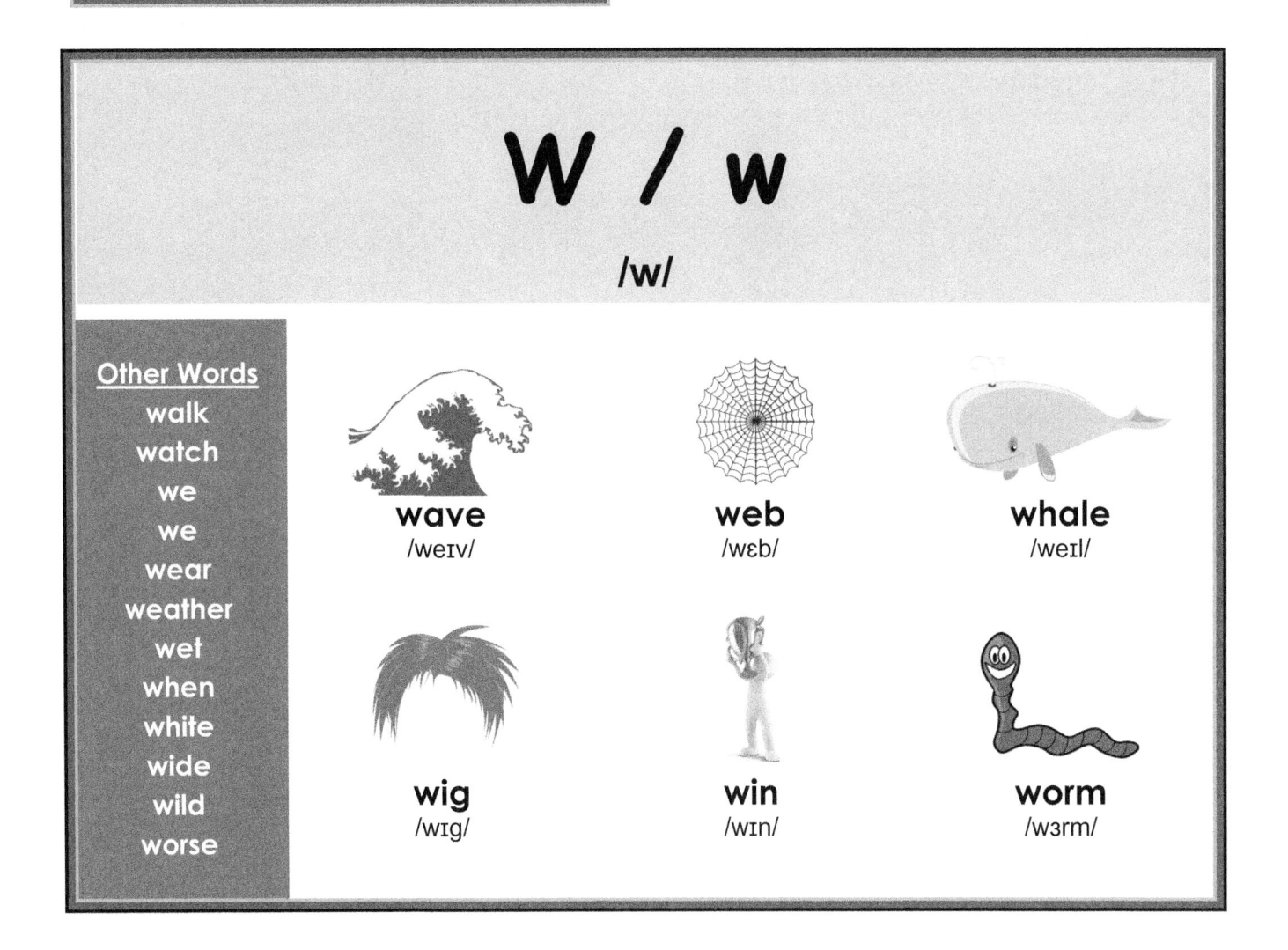

W / w
/w/

Other Words
walk
watch
we
we
wear
weather
wet
when
white
wide
wild
worse

wave /weɪv/

web /wɛb/

whale /weɪl/

wig /wɪg/

win /wɪn/

worm /wɜrm/

Part 5B: Write and read

1. __e __atch __et __hales __ear __igs.

2. __eather is __orse __hen __hite __orms __in.

3. __alk __ide of __ebs and __ild __aves.

Part 6: Fun review

Unscramble the sentences

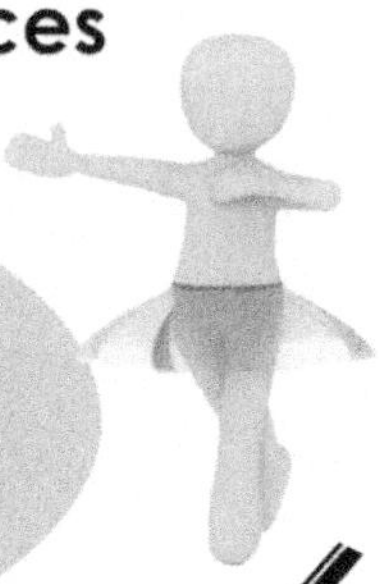

1. Yes, she is. She's wearing a skirt.

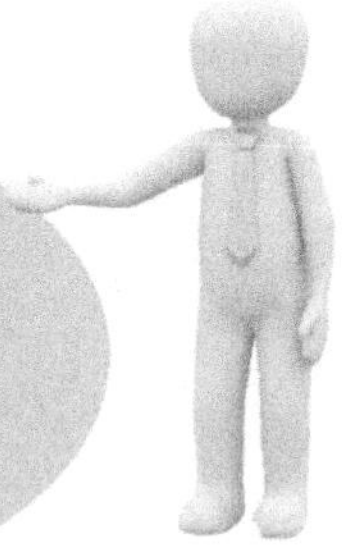

2. _____
   _____

3. _____

4. _____
   _____

5. _____

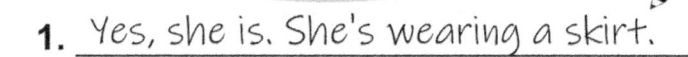

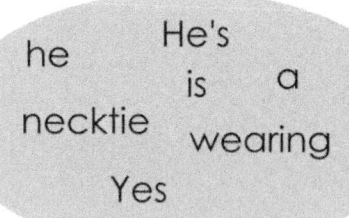

Complete the words and match

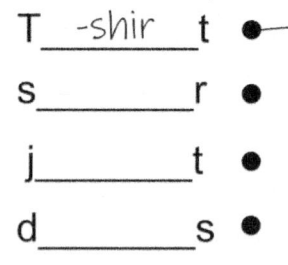

T_-shir_t •

s_____r •

j_____t •

d_____s •

Lesson 13: Countries

países

Part 1A: Learn the words

1. **Argentina**
   Argentina
2. **Australia**
   Austrália
3. **Brazil**
   Brasil
4. **Canada**
   Canadá
5. **China**
   China
6. **Japan**
   Japão
7. **Kenya**
   Quênia
8. **Mexico**
   México
9. **New Zealand**
   Nova Zelândia
10. **South Africa**
    África do Sul

⭐ Practice speaking: "<u>África do Sul</u>" means "<u>South Africa</u>"! ⭐

Part 1B: Write the words

Write the missing letters!   Write x 1   Write x 2

1. A _ g _ n _ i _ a
2. _ u _ t _ a _ i _
3. B _ a _ i _
4. _ a _ a _ a
5. C _ i _ a
6. _ a _ a _
7. K _ n _ a
8. _ e _ i _ o
9. N _ w _ e _ l _ n _
10. _ o _ t _ A _ r _ c _

Part 2A: Ask a question

Where are you going?

✓ We're going to <u>Australia</u>. We're not going to <u>China</u>.

Where's she going?

✓ She's going to <u>Brazil</u>. She isn't going to <u>Kenya</u>.

⭐ **Winner's Tip!** where's = where is

Part 2B: Fill in the blanks

1. Where _____ you _____?
   I'm _____ to _____. I'm not going to Canada.

2. _____ are _____ going?
   They're going to _____. They _____ going to Mexico.

3. Where's _____ _____?
   She's _____ to _____. She _____ going to China.

4. _____ _____ _____?
   He's going to _____. He _____ _____ to Japan.

Part 3A: Yes / No questions

Are they going to Canada?

✓ **Yes, they are. They're going to Canada.**
✗ **No, they're not. They're not going to Canada.**

Is he going to Mexico?

✓ **Yes, he is. He's going to Mexico.**
✗ **No, he isn't. He isn't going to Mexico.**

⭐ **Winner's Tip!** He isn't = He's not, etc.

Part 3B: Fill in the blanks

1. _____ you _____ to New Zealand?
   Yes, I _____. I'm _____ to _____.

2. _____ she _____ to _____?
   No, _____ isn't. She _____ going to Argentina.

3. Is _____ _____ to _____?
   No, he isn't. _____ isn't _____ to South Africa.

4. Are _____ _____ _____ Brazil?
   Yes, we _____. We're _____ _____ Brazil.

Part 4A: Verb of the day

write / writes – wrote – writing – written (escrever)

Every evening, I <u>write</u> things in my journal.

She usually <u>writes</u> stories to tell her niece.

Last year, he <u>wrote</u> a book about travel.

We are <u>writing</u> about our feelings right now.

They have never <u>written</u> any English words.

Part 4B: Verb Practice

1. Every afternoon, I _____ down my ideas for dinner.
2. On Thursdays, she _____ on paper at her desk.
3. Every week, he _____ about different countries.
4. Last class, we _____ homework about Australia.
5. Last week, I _____ a letter to my friend in Japan.
6. Earlier today, we _____ down some ideas on Canada.
7. Right now, she is _____ to her family in Argentina.
8. We are _____ in the English class right now.
9. He has never _____ any good stories before.
10. We have _____ down a lot of information already.

Part 5A: Phonics Practice

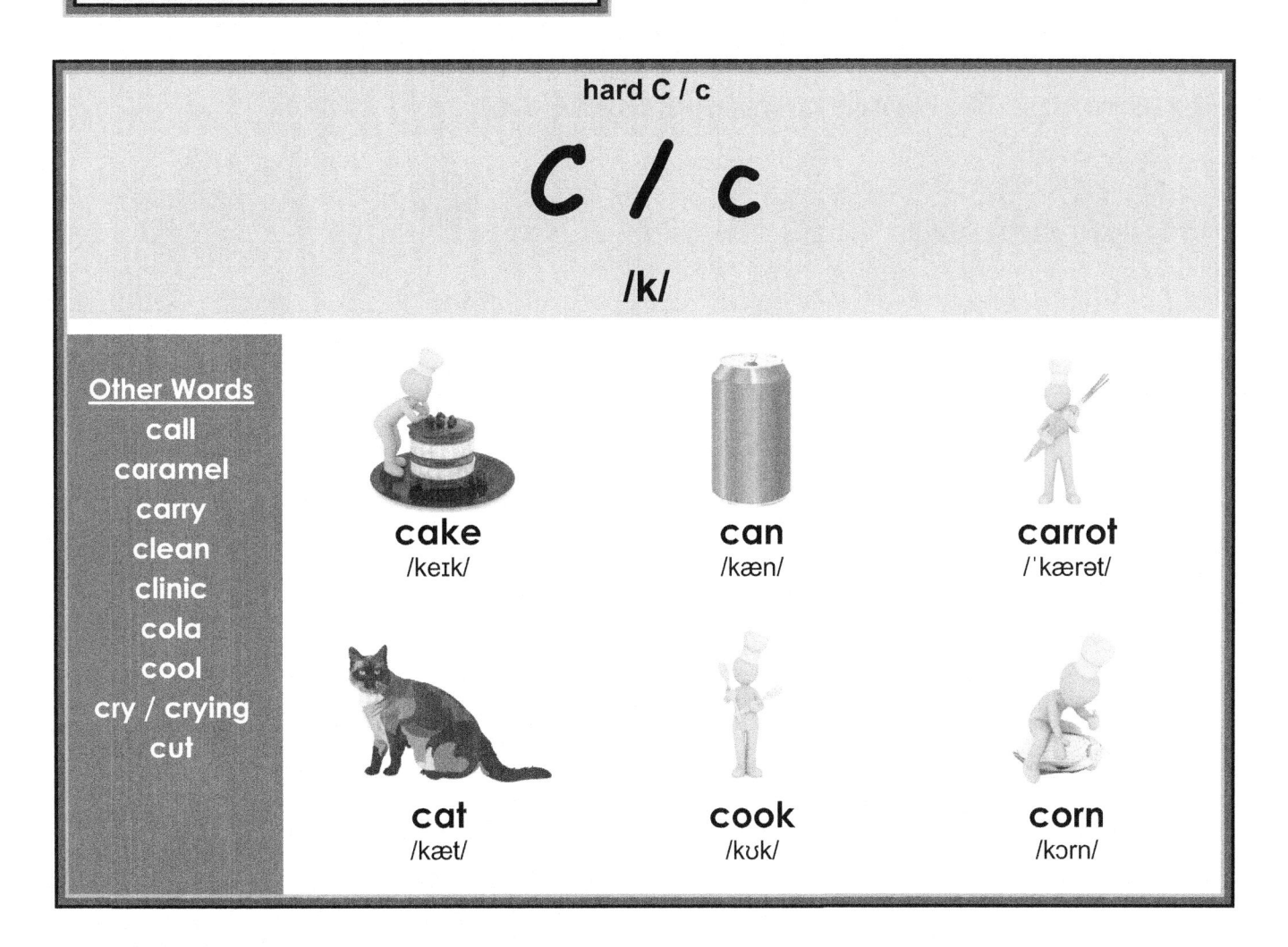

hard C / c
C / c
/k/

Other Words
- call
- caramel
- carry
- clean
- clinic
- cola
- cool
- cry / crying
- cut

cake /keɪk/

can /kæn/

carrot /ˈkærət/

cat /kæt/

cook /kʊk/

corn /kɔrn/

Part 5B: Write and read

1. __ool __ooks __ut __aramel __ake.

2. __rying __ats __an __all __lean __lini__s.

3. __arry __orn, __arrots and __ola __ans.

Part 6: Fun review

Unscramble the words and write the sentences

alizrb — Brazil
aandac — Canada
najpa — _____
shuot cfaira — _____

1. He 's going to Brazil.
   He isn't going to Canada.

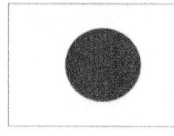

2. They _____

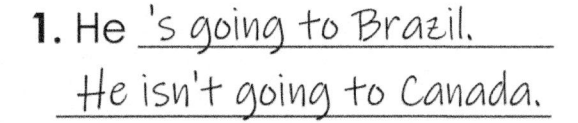

3. yaekn _____

4. etganrian _____

5. coiexm _____ iulrstaaa _____

   We _____

6. niahc _____ ewn aaelnzd _____

   She _____

82

Lesson 14: Places

locais

Part 1A: Learn the words

1. **beach**
   praia
2. **cinema**
   cinema
3. **department store**
   department store
4. **gym**
   academia
5. **night market**
   mercado noturno
6. **park**
   parque
7. **restaurant**
   restaurante
8. **store**
   loja
9. **supermarket**
   supermercado
10. **swimming pool**
    a piscina

⭐ Practice speaking: "_Praia_" means "_beach_"! ⭐

Part 1B: Write the words

Write the missing letters!   Write x 1   Write x 2

1. b _ a _ h
2. _ i _ e _ a
3. d _ p _ rtm _ nt   st _ re
4. _ y _
5. n _ g _ t   _ a _ k _ t
6. p _ r _
7. _ e _ t _ u _ a _ t
8. s _ o _ e
9. _ u _ e _ m _ r _ e _
10. s _ i _ m _ n _   p _ ol

Part 2A: Ask a question

Who are you going to the <u>restaurant</u> with?

✓ I'm going to the restaurant with my <u>brother</u>.
✗ I'm not going to the restaurant with my <u>sister</u>.

Who's she going to the <u>beach</u> with?

✓ She's going to the beach with her <u>cousin</u>.
✗ She's not going to the beach with her <u>uncle</u>.

⭐ **Winner's Tip!** who's = who is

Part 2B: Fill in the blanks

1. _____ are _____ going to the _____ with?
   I'm _____ to the park _____ my _____.

2. Who's he _____ to the cinema _____?
   _____ not going to the _____ with _____ sister.

3. _____ are _____ going to the restaurant with?
   They're _____ to the _____ with his _____.

4. _____ she _____ to _____ gym _____?
   _____ going _____ the _____ with her brother.

Part 3A: Yes / No questions

Are we going to the store with my aunt?

✓ **Yes, we are. We're going to the store with her.**
✗ **No, we're not. We're not going there with your aunt.**

Is she going to the gym with your father?

✓ **Yes, she is. She's going to the gym with my father.**
✗ **No, she isn't. She isn't going there with him.**

⭐ **Winner's Tip!** my, your, his, her, its, our, their

Part 3B: Fill in the blanks

1. Are you _____ to the store _____ your uncle?
   No, I'm not. I'm _____ going _____ with him.

2. Is _____ going to the park with your _____?
   No, he _____. He isn't _____ there with her.

3. _____ we going to the gym _____ my aunt?
   No, we _____. We aren't _____ there with her.

4. Is _____ going to the store with her _____?
   Yes, _____ is. She's _____ _____ with him.

Part 4A: Verb of the day

walk / walks – walked – walking – walked (andar)

Every morning, we <u>walk</u> to school together.

He usually <u>walks</u> in the park each afternoon.

Yesterday, they <u>walked</u> home from the store.

She is <u>walking</u> to the gym with him right now.

I have never <u>walked</u> very far at the beach.

Part 4B: Verb Practice

1. Every evening, they _____ around the night market.
2. On Tuesdays, she _____ to the department store.
3. Every weekend, he _____ to the swimming pool.
4. Yesterday, we _____ home from the supermarket.
5. Last weekend, I _____ to many different places.
6. Last night, she _____ for a long time at the park.
7. Right now, he is _____ from the store to the gym.
8. I am _____ at the zoo right now with my friend.
9. He has never _____ very much in his life.
10. You have _____ to almost every place in this city.

Part 5A: Phonics Practice

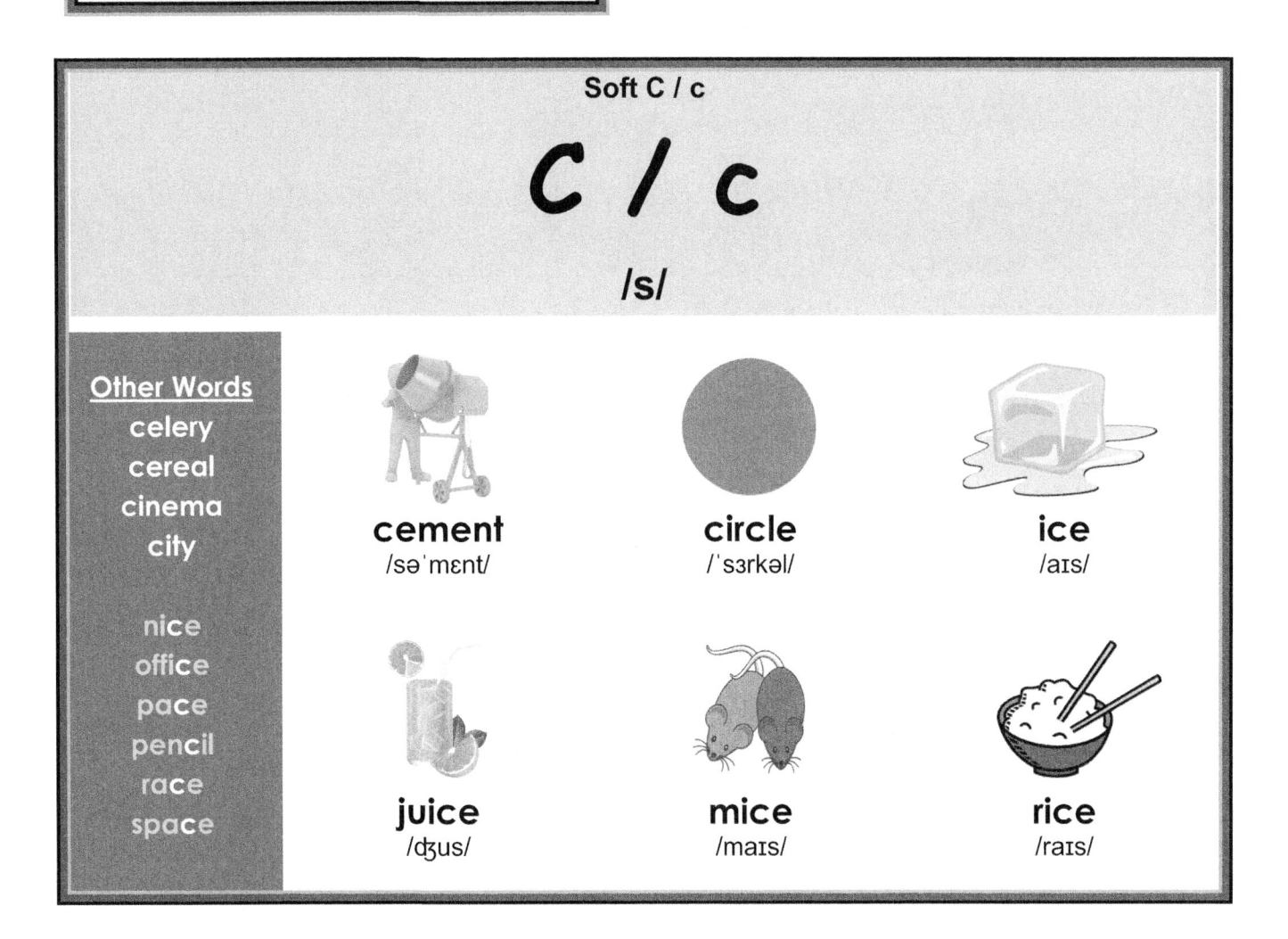

Soft C / c

C / c

/s/

Other Words
celery
cereal
cinema
city

nice
office
pace
pencil
race
space

cement
/səˈmɛnt/

circle
/ˈsɜrkəl/

ice
/aɪs/

juice
/dʒus/

mice
/maɪs/

rice
/raɪs/

Part 5B: Write and read

1. __inema mi__e ra__e __ircles pa__ing i__e.

2. Jui__e, ri__e, __elery and __ereal taste ni__e.

3. __ement __ity offi__e spa__e sells pen__ils.

Part 6: Fun review

Write the answers

1. Who are you going to the cinema with?
   <u>I'm going to the cinema with her cousin.</u>
   her cousin

2. Who is he going to the gym with?  
   _____
   my brother

3. Who is she going to the restaurant with?
   _____
   your sister

4. Who are they going to the park with?  
   _____
   his niece

Write the questions

1. <u>Are you going to the swimming pool with his aunt?</u>
   Yes, I am. I'm going to the swimming pool with his aunt.

2. _____
   No, he isn't. He's not going to the store with my grandfather.

3. _____
   Yes, we are. We're going to the park with her father.

Lesson 15: Transportation

transporte

Part 1A: Learn the words

1. take an **airplane**
   pegue um avião
2. ride a **bicycle**
   andar de bicicleta
3. catch a **bus**
   pegar um ônibus
4. drive a **car**
   dirigir um carro
5. take a **ferry**
   pegue uma balsa
6. ride a **motorcycle**
   andar de motocicleta
7. ride a **scooter**
   andar de scooter
8. take the **subway**
   pegue um metro
9. take a **taxi**
   pegar um táxi
10. take a **train**
    pegue um trem

★ Practice speaking: "_Pegue um trem_" means "_take a train_"! ★

Part 1B: Write the words

Write the missing letters!   Write x 1   Write x 2

1. _i_p_a_e
2. b_c_c_e
3. _u_
4. _a_
5. f_r_y
6. _o_o_c_c_e
7. s_o_t_r
8. _u_w_y
9. t_x_
10. _r_i_

89

Part 2A: Ask a question

How do you get to the department store?

✓ I <u>catch a bus</u> to get to the department store.
✗ I don't <u>take a taxi</u> to get there.

How does he get to the beach?

✓ He <u>takes an airplane</u> to get to the beach.
✗ He doesn't <u>take a ferry</u> to get there.

★ **Winner's Tip!** Answer with "there" for the <u>place</u>

Part 2B: Fill in the blanks

1. _____ do you _____ to the _____?
   I _____ to get _____ the beach.

2. How _____ he get to _____ restaurant?
   He doesn't _____ to _____ there.

3. How _____ she _____ to the _____?
   She _____ to _____ _____ the gym.

4. _____ do _____ get to the _____?
   They _____ to _____ to _____ store.

90

Part 3A: Yes / No questions

Do you <u>ride a scooter</u> to get to the <u>swimming pool</u>?

✓ **Yes, I do.** I ride a scooter **to get** there.
✗ **No, I don't.** I don't ride a scooter **to get** there.

Does he <u>take the subway</u> to get to the <u>cinema</u>?

✓ **Yes, he does.** He takes the subway **to get** there.
✗ **No, he doesn't.** He doesn't take the subway **to get** there.

⭐ **Winner's Tip!** Remember: he / she / it verb + s

Part 3B: Fill in the blanks

1. Do _____ _____ to get to _____ park?
   Yes, I do. I ride a bicycle to _____ to the _____.

2. Does he _____ to _____ to the beach?
   No, he _____. He _____ take a taxi to get there.

3. Do _____ _____ to get to the swimming pool?
   Yes, we _____. We take the subway to get _____.

4. Does she _____ to _____ to the store?
   Yes, she _____. She _____ to get _____.

Part 4A: Verb of the day

visit / visits – visited – visiting – visited (visitar)

Every year, you <u>visit</u> your family in Paris.

He usually <u>visits</u> us in the late afternoon.

Yesterday, I <u>visited</u> her at the beach.

They are <u>visiting</u> from Europe right now.

We have never <u>visited</u> another country.

Part 4B: Verb Practice

1. Every summer, I _____ my family living in America.
2. On weekends, she _____ her sick grandmother.
3. Every Sunday, he _____ the library and reads books.
4. Last winter, they _____ Europe and went skiing.
5. Last weekend, I _____ my friend in the hospital.
6. Last spring, we _____ an amazing national park.
7. Right now, he is _____ his cousins in the city.
8. We are _____ with my aunt and uncle right now.
9. She has never _____ Asia or Australia before.
10. I have _____ many incredible countries so far.

Part 5A: Phonics Practice

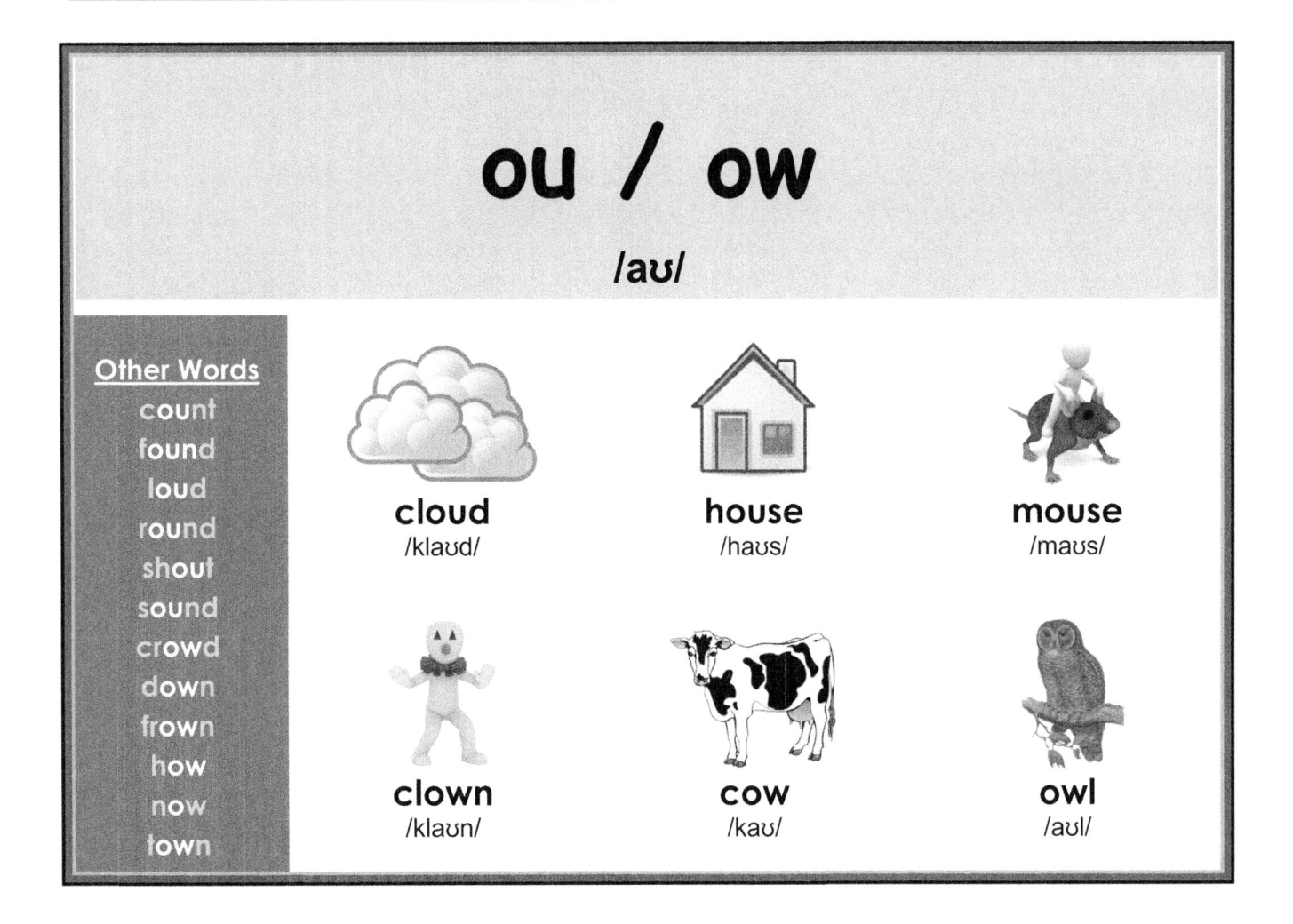

ou / ow
/aʊ/

Other Words
count
found
loud
round
shout
sound
crowd
down
frown
how
now
town

cloud /klaʊd/

house /haʊs/

mouse /maʊs/

clown /klaʊn/

cow /kaʊ/

owl /aʊl/

Part 5B: Write and read

1. D___n cl___ns f___nd h___ c___s fr___n.

2. N___ r___nd ___ls c___nt l___d cr___ds.

3. T___n h___se m___se sh___ts cl___d s___nds.

Part 6: Fun review

Catch, drive, ride, or take? Choose a place, write sentences

drive	She _drives a car to get to the beach._
_____	We _____
_____	They _____
_____	You _____
_____	He _____
_____	I _____

Write questions

_____	_Does_ she _take a train to get to Mexico?_
_____	_____ he _____
_____	_____ you _____
_____	_____ we _____

Winner's Tip - Places: park, beach, night market, store, supermarket, restaurant, swimming pool, department store, cinema, gym, (country names)

TEST 3: Lessons 11 - 15

Write the correct answer next to the letter "A"

A: ___ 1. Where _____ the penguins? The penguins are _____ the lion.
a) is / next to
b) are / between
c) is / across from
d) are / near

A: ___ 2. What are you _____? I'm not _____ a hat.
a) wearing / wear
b) wearing / wearing
c) wore / wear
d) wears / worn

A: ___ 3. _____ she going? She's _____ to Japan.
a) Where / gone
b) Where are / go
c) Where's / going
d) Where is / went

A: ___ 4. _____ are all _____ to the supermarket right now.
a) We / walk
b) They / walking
c) You / walked
d) They're / walking

A: ___ 5. How do you _____ to the restaurant? I take a taxi to get _____.
a) get / there
b) go / restaurant
c) go / to restaurant
d) getting / to there

A: ___ 6. Do you _____ an airplane to _____ your family?
a) ride / visit
b) take / visited
c) catch / visiting
d) take / visit

A: ___ 7. He usually _____ to the cinema after _____ work.
a) walks / his
b) walking / he
c) walk / done
d) walked / did

A: ___ 8. Are we _____ to Kenya? Yes, we are. _____ going to Kenya.
a) going / We're
b) go / We are
c) going / We've
d) gone / We

A: ___ 9. Is he _____ a T-shirt? Yes, he is. _____ wearing a T-shirt.
a) wear / He is
b) wears / He
c) wearing / He's
d) worn / He has

95

A: ___ 10. Is the rhino _____ the bear? No, it _____. It isn't next to the bear.
a) near / don't
b) between / doesn't
c) across from / not
d) next to / isn't

A: ___ 11. My mother _____ a letter to her friend in China last _____.
a) wrote / month
b) writes / week
c) write / year
d) writing / time

A: ___ 12. I usually _____ a bicycle to _____ my friend at the beach.
a) take / visiting
b) ride / visit
c) catch / visited
d) ride / visits

A: ___ 13. _____ always _____ the giraffes at the zoo.
a) They / like
b) We / likes
c) You / liking
d) She / like

A: ___ 14. Who are you _____ to the swimming pool with? I'm going to the swimming pool _____ my uncle.
a) going / by
b) go / for
c) going / with
d) goes / to

A: ___ 15. He _____ never _____ a necktie to the office.
a) is / wear
b) have / wore
c) has / worn
d) has / wearing

A: ___ 16. Where _____ they going? _____ going to China.
a) is / They
b) 're / They are
c) have / They've
d) are / They're

A: ___ 17. I _____ never _____ monkeys very much.
a) am / liking
b) have / liked
c) have / likes
d) am / liked

A: ___ 18. Is she going to the store with your nephew? Yes, she is. She's going _____ with _____.
a) to store / nephew
b) there / him
c) in / her
d) there / her

Answers on page 129

Lesson 16: Meats

carnes

Part 1A: Learn the words

1. **bacon**
   bacon
2. **beef**
   carne de vaca
3. **chicken**
   carne de frango
4. **fish**
   peixe
5. **ham**
   presunto
6. **lamb**
   carne de cordeiro
7. **pork**
   carne de porco
8. **salami**
   salame
9. **sausage**
   linguiça
10. **shrimp**
    camarão

⭐ Practice speaking: "_Carne de frango_" is "_chicken_" in English! ⭐

Part 1B: Write the words

Write the missing letters!   Write x 1   Write x 2

1. b__c__n
2. __e__f
3. c__i__k__n
4. __i__h
5. __a__
6. l__m__
7. __o__k
8. s__l__m__
9. __a__s__g__
10. s__r__m__

Part 2A: Ask a question

What kind of meat did you eat for <u>dinner</u>?

✓ **We ate <u>shrimp</u> for dinner. We didn't eat <u>ham</u>.**

What kind of meat did he eat for <u>lunch</u>?

✓ **He ate <u>beef</u> for lunch. He didn't eat <u>fish</u>.**

⭐ **Winner's Tip!** Learn: breakfast, lunch, dinner, a snack

Part 2B: Fill in the blanks

1. What _____ of _____ did you _____ for lunch?
   I _____ ham. I _____ eat _____.

2. What _____ of _____ did she _____ for dinner?
   _____ _____ pork. She _____ eat lamb.

3. _____ kind of meat _____ he eat for _____?
   He ate _____. He _____ _____ salami.

4. _____ kind of meat _____ they eat for _____?
   They _____ beef. _____ _____ _____ shrimp.

Part 3A: Yes / No questions

Did you eat sausage for breakfast?

✓ **Yes, I did. I ate** sausage **for breakfast.**
✗ **No, I didn't. I didn't eat** sausage **for breakfast.**

Did she eat chicken for a snack?

✓ **Yes, she did. She ate** chicken **for a snack.**
✗ **No, she didn't. She didn't eat** chicken **for a snack.**

⭐ **Winner's Tip!** didn't = did not

Part 3B: Fill in the blanks

1. _____ you eat _____ for lunch?
   Yes, I _____. I _____ lamb for _____.

2. Did _____ eat _____ for _____?
   No, she _____. She _____ eat pork for a snack.

3. Did _____ _____ bacon for _____?
   No, they _____. They _____ eat bacon for lunch.

4. Did _____ _____ _____ for _____?
   Yes, he did. He _____ _____ for _____.

Part 4A: Verb of the day

eat / eats – ate – eating – eaten (comer)

Every morning, we <u>eat</u> bacon for breakfast.

Sometimes, she <u>eats</u> too much meat.

Yesterday, they <u>ate</u> lunch with my family.

He is <u>eating</u> a pizza with his brother now.

We have never <u>eaten</u> food from Japan.

Part 4B: Verb Practice

1. Daily, she _____ many different vegetables.
2. On Thursdays, we _____ at a restaurant nearby.
3. Every Tuesday, he _____ with me at the park.
4. Last week, he _____ some great Chinese food.
5. Yesterday, I _____ a delicious cake with my friend.
6. Last time, we _____ some grapes and cherries.
7. Right now, she is _____ some tasty apple pie.
8. They are _____ many kinds of meat right now.
9. He has never _____ shrimp or fish before.
10. I have _____ many kinds of fruits this week.

Part 5A: Phonics Practice

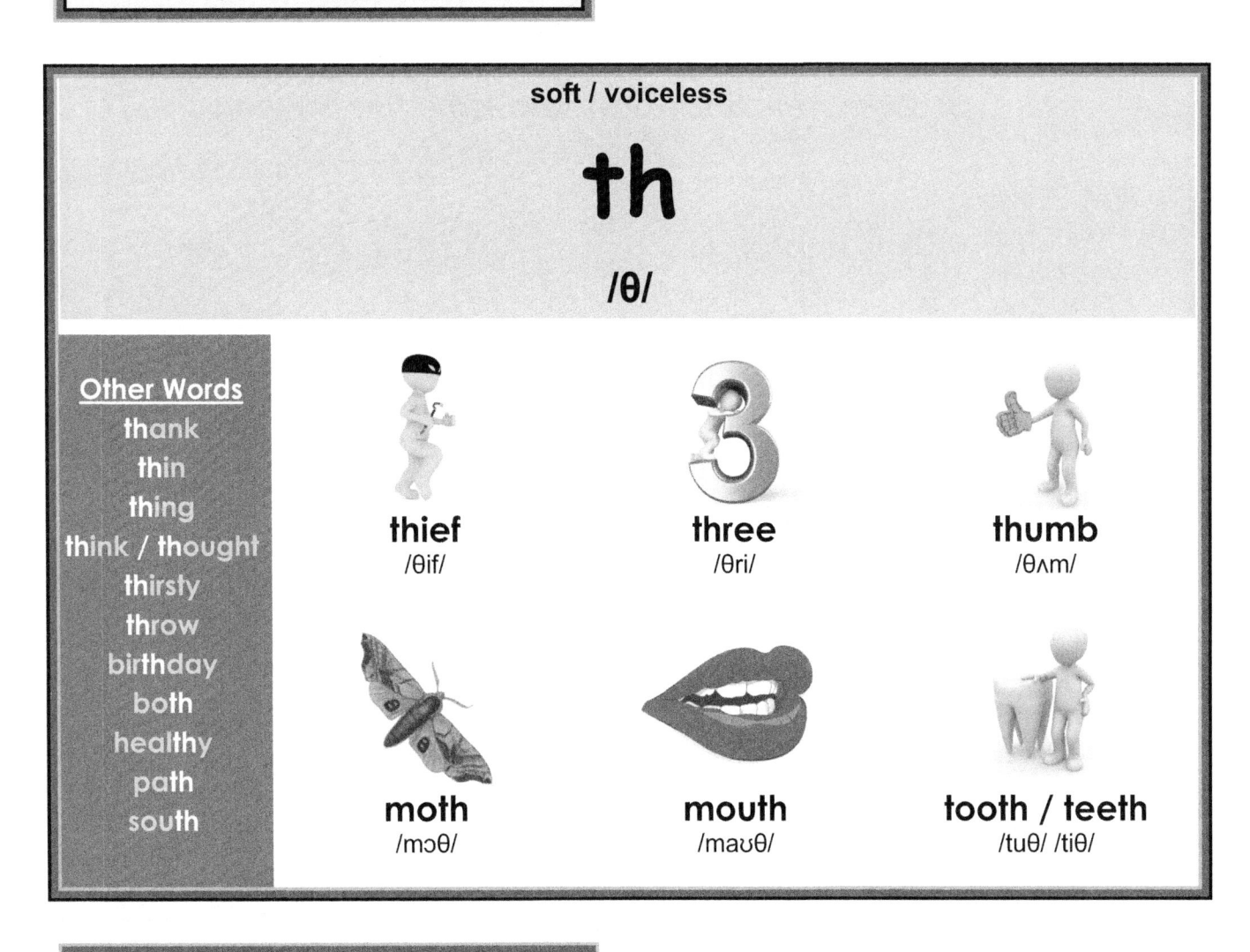

soft / voiceless

th

/θ/

Other Words
thank
thin
thing
think / thought
thirsty
throw
birthday
both
healthy
path
south

thief /θif/

three /θri/

thumb /θʌm/

moth /mɔθ/

mouth /maʊθ/

tooth / teeth /tuθ/ /tiθ/

Part 5B: Write and read

1. A heal___y ___in ___ief ___rows ___ree ___ings.

2. A ___irsty mo___ mou___ ___anks tee___.

3. Bo___ bir___day ___umbs ___ink sou___ pa___.

Part 6: Fun review

Complete the words and write the answers

p o r k

□ r □ □

□ □ □ s □ □ □

□ □ □ f

□ □ □ h

□ □ □ □ e □

□ □ c □ □

□
a
□
□

p o r k

□ a □

□ □ □ □ m □

Lesson 17: At school

na escola

Part 1A: Learn the words

1. **art room**
   sala de arte
2. **classroom**
   sala de aula
3. **computer lab**
   laboratório de informática
4. **gym**
   ginásio
5. **hall**
   auditório
6. **lunchroom**
   sala de almoço
7. **music room**
   sala de musica
8. **nurse's office**
   escritório da enfermeira
9. **office**
   escritório
10. **science lab**
    laboratório de ciências

⭐ Practice speaking: "_Sala de almoço_" is "_lunchroom_" in English! ⭐

Part 1B: Write the words

Write the missing letters!   Write x 1   Write x 2

1. _ r _   r _ o _
2. c _ a _ s _ o _ m
3. _ o _ p _ t _ r   l _ b
4. _ y _
5. h _ l _
6. _ u _ c _ r _ o _
7. m _ s _ c   _ o _ m
8. _ u _ s _ 's   _ f _ i _ e
9. o _ f _ c _
10. _ c _ e _ c _   l _ b

Part 2A: Ask a question

Where did you see the teacher yesterday?

✓ Yesterday, **I saw the** teacher **in the** office.
✗ Yesterday, **I didn't see the** teacher **in the** hall.

Where did she see the principal last week?

✓ Last week, **she saw the** principal **in the** science lab.
✗ Last week, **she didn't see the** principal **in the** art room.

⭐ **Winner's Tip!** Learn: yesterday, last week, last month

Part 2B: Fill in the blanks

1. where _____ he _____ the teacher _____?
   Last week, he _____ the teacher in the _____.

2. where _____ she _____ the principal _____?
   Yesterday, she _____ see the _____ in the hall.

3. _____ did _____ see the _____ last month?
   _____, I saw the coach _____ the _____.

4. _____ _____ he see the _____ yesterday?
   Yesterday, he _____ see the _____ in the _____.

Part 3A: Yes / No questions

Did he see a <u>classmate</u> in the <u>art room</u> <u>last week</u>?

✓ **Yes, he did.** He saw a classmate there last week.
✗ **No, he didn't.** He didn't see a classmate there last week.

Did they see a <u>coach</u> in the <u>gym</u> <u>yesterday</u>?

✓ **Yes, they did.** They saw a coach there yesterday.
✗ **No, they didn't.** They didn't see a coach there yesterday.

⭐ **Winner's Tip!** Learn: teacher, principal, coach, classmate

Part 3B: Fill in the blanks

1. Did you see a _____ in the gym _____?
   Yes, I _____. I _____ a teacher there yesterday.

2. _____ she see a _____ in the office _____?
   Yes, she did. She _____ a coach there last week.

3. Did he _____ a classmate in the hall _____?
   No, he didn't. He didn't see a _____ there last month.

4. Did we see a _____ in the _____ _____?
   Yes, _____ did. We saw a _____ there _____.

Part 4A: Verb of the day

put / puts – put – putting – put (pôr)

Every day, I <u>put</u> my books in the office.

He usually <u>puts</u> pencils in the art room.

Yesterday, he <u>put</u> some balls in the gym.

She is <u>putting</u> chairs in the music room.

He has never <u>put</u> anything in the hall.

Part 4B: Verb Practice

1. Each day, he _____ some papers in the office.
2. On Fridays, she _____ some fruit in the lunchroom.
3. Every Monday, I _____ a blue T-shirt in my bag.
4. Yesterday, he _____ some milk in his coffee.
5. Last time, we _____ more cheese on our pizza.
6. Last week, she _____ some books on the bookshelf.
7. Right now, she is _____ some drinks in the car.
8. They are _____ some toys with the monkeys.
9. I have never _____ fruit into a salad before.
10. He has _____ meat in his lunches for many years.

Part 5A: Phonics Practice

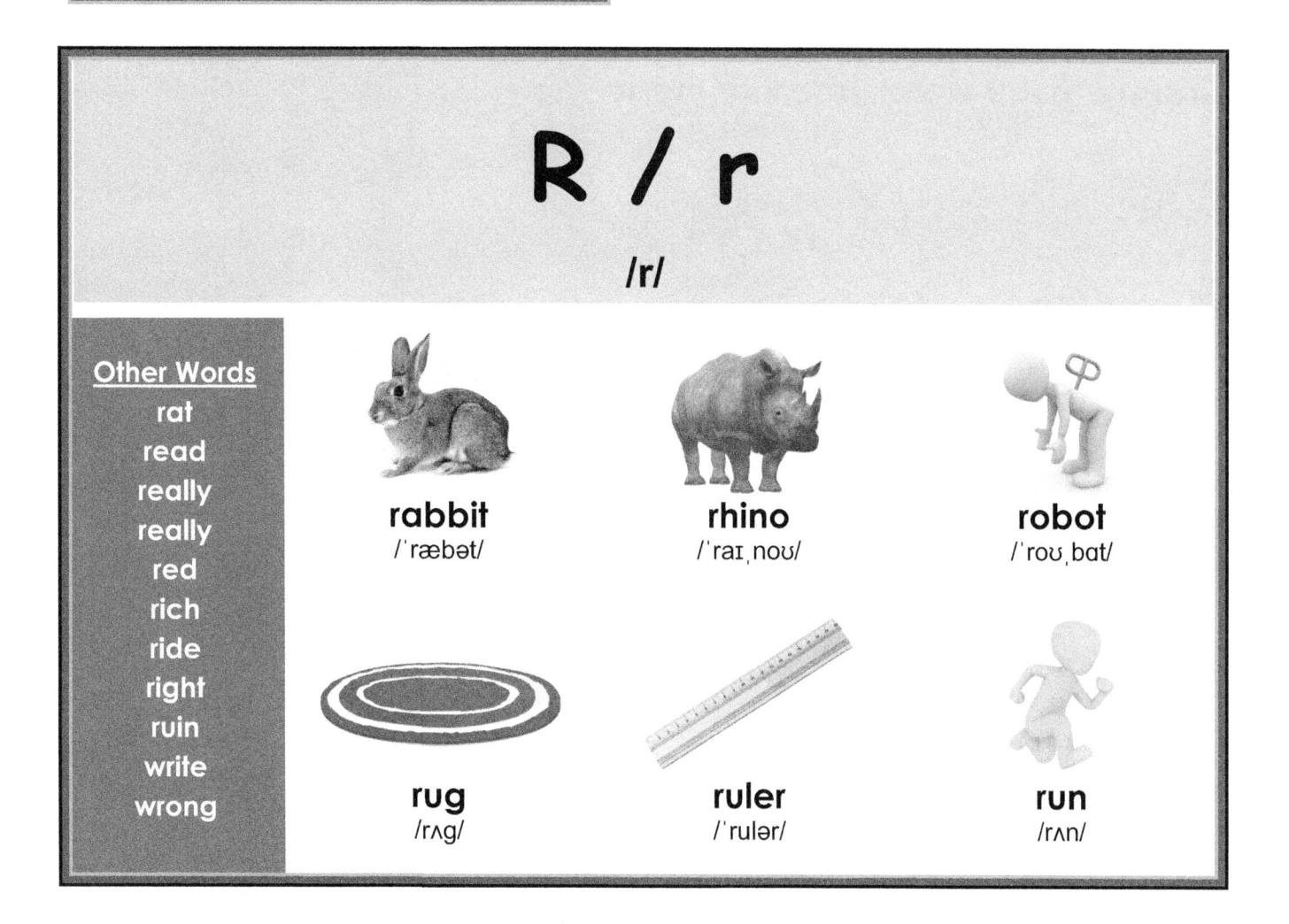

R / r
/r/

Other Words
rat
read
really
really
red
rich
ride
right
ruin
write
wrong

rabbit
/ˈræbət/

rhino
/ˈraɪˌnoʊ/

robot
/ˈroʊˌbɑt/

rug
/rʌg/

ruler
/ˈrulər/

run
/rʌn/

Part 5B: Write and read

1. __ed __abbits __ide __obot __hinos __ight.

2. W__ong __ulers __eally __uin __ugs.

3. __eally __ich __ats __ead, __un and w__ite.

Part 6: Fun review

Complete the words and find them

g_y_m

c_____m

a____ ____m

```
g s o f f i c e f m b t x s v m x v
y e s t e r d a y d i x h h m m e t
m w u h r r v s x y n u x o q t b o
w t e a c h e r p s p o o b a m m b
c o m p u t e r l a b r v m m g e p
b d k s l i v r d r t g s u p c f u
w e c c a y r l r t s m g i x y t
y t z i s h j i a u a m s f k p i t
k b q e t u d g b l z e f h h l w i
p k o n m l u n c h r o o m a j w n
x p s c o m e x b k s x w p l e d g
r o n e n y g o g e v m i j l p u t
f i b l t s b h s y b c v e f t o a
a n m a h o m r g h n v o e n g p e
a e u b v u u u h i l a s t w e e k
f e b w i n n e r s e n g l i s h h
o y w d a v x p i b a t s c h o o l
v v j e c o a c h m r e r s h f o m
```

o_____e

l_____m

h_____l

s_____b

m_____m

n_____e

c_____b

" <u>Last month</u>, I saw the <u>coach</u> in the <u>gym.</u> "

Lesson 18: More clothes

mais roupas

Part 1A: Learn the words

1. **boots**
   chuteiras
2. **dresses**
   vestidos
3. **gloves**
   luvas
4. **jeans**
   jeans
5. **pajamas**
   pijamas
6. **pants**
   calça
7. **shirts**
   camisa
8. **shoes**
   sapatos
9. **shorts**
   calção
10. **socks**
    meias

⭐ Practice speaking: "_Sapatos_" is "_shoes_" in English! ⭐

Part 1B: Write the words

Write the missing letters!   Write x 1   Write x 2

1. __o__t__
2. d__e__s__s
3. __l__v__s
4. j__a__s
5. __a__a__a__
6. p__n__s
7. __h__r__s
8. s__o__s
9. __h__r__s
10. s__c__s

Part 2A: Ask a question

Where did you buy these <u>gloves</u>?

✓ I bought these gloves <u>at the department store</u>.
✗ I didn't buy them <u>at the shopping mall</u>.

Where did she buy those <u>dresses</u>?

✓ She bought those dresses <u>online</u>.
✗ She didn't buy them <u>at the store</u>.

⭐ **Winner's Tip!** Learn: online

Part 2B: Fill in the blanks

1. where _____ he _____ those pajamas?
   He _____ those _____ at the department store.

2. _____ _____ she buy these _____?
   _____ bought _____ dresses online.

3. _____ _____ you buy those _____?
   I _____ buy _____ at the store.

4. _____ _____ they _____ those _____?
   _____ didn't _____ _____ online.

Part 3A: Yes / No questions

Did he buy these <u>pants</u> in <u>Japan</u>?

✓ **Yes, he did. He bought these** pants **in** Japan.
✗ **No, he didn't. He didn't buy** them there.

Did we buy those <u>socks</u> in <u>Canada</u>?

✓ **Yes, we did. We bought those** socks **in** Canada.
✗ **No, we didn't. We didn't buy** them there.

⭐ **Winner's Tip!** Answer with "them" for plural nouns

Part 3B: Fill in the blanks

1. Did _____ buy those _____ in _____?
   Yes, she did. She _____ _____ shorts in Korea.

2. Did _____ _____ these shoes _____ China?
   No, he _____. He didn't buy them _____.

3. Did _____ buy those jeans in _____?
   No, _____ _____. They didn't _____ them there.

4. Did _____ buy _____ _____ in _____?
   Yes, I _____. I _____ _____ boots in Mexico.

Part 4A: Verb of the day

lend / lends – lent – lending – lent (emprestar)

Every day, I <u>lend</u> money to my friend.

Sometimes, she <u>lends</u> me her bicycle.

Yesterday, he <u>lent</u> her some socks.

He is <u>lending</u> us some green pencils.

I have never <u>lent</u> anything to him.

Part 4B: Verb Practice

1. Every class, I _____ my classmate a colored pen.
2. On Thursdays, she _____ a board game to us.
3. Every week, he _____ his car to his brother.
4. Last time, they _____ him a toy dinosaur.
5. Last weekend, I _____ a book to my best friend.
6. Yesterday, we _____ some glue to her sister.
7. Right now, she is _____ us some markers and tape.
8. We are _____ him some clothes for the party.
9. She has never _____ money to her niece.
10. You have _____ many toys to people this month.

Part 5A: Phonics Practice

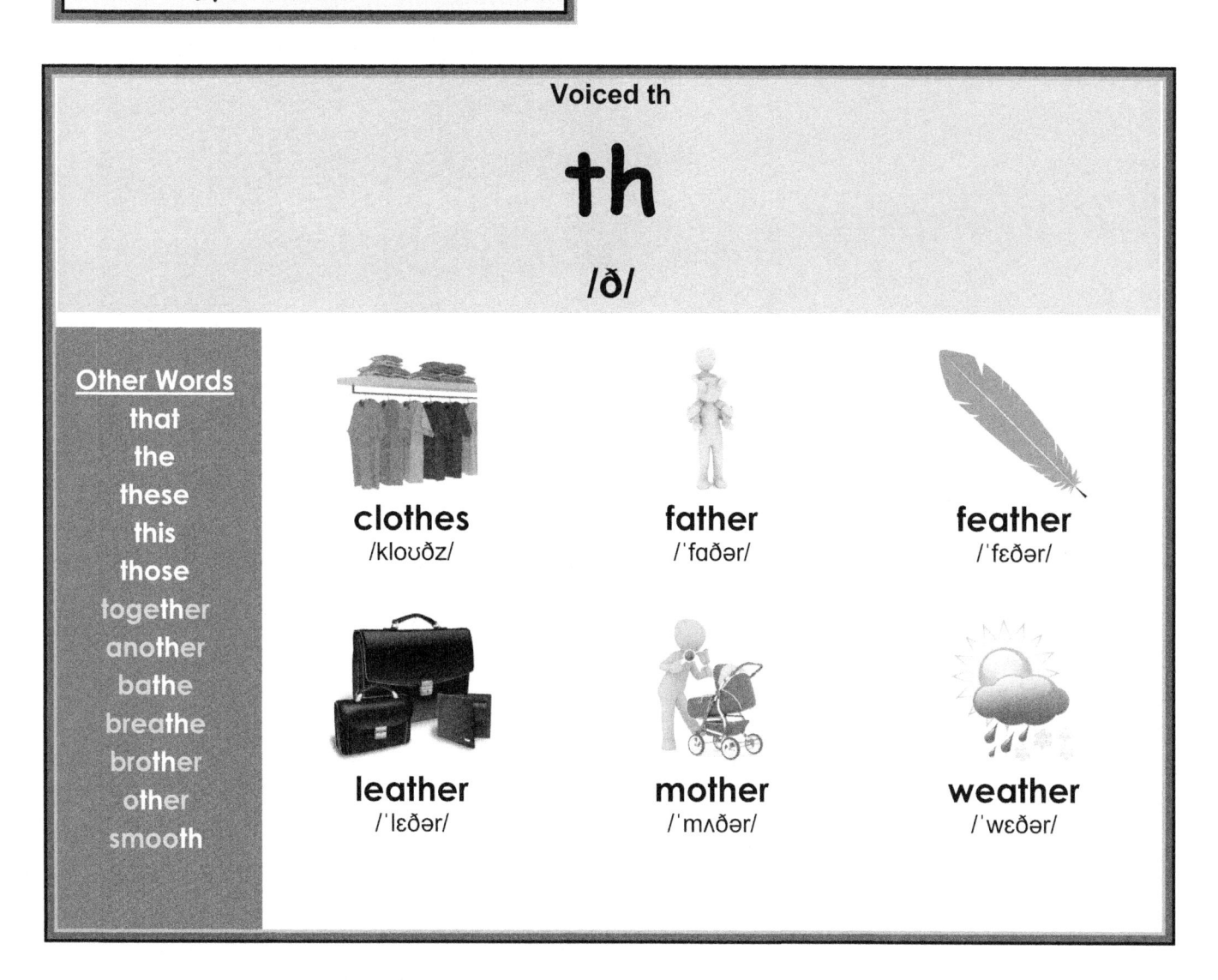

Voiced th

th
/ð/

Other Words
that
the
these
this
those
together
another
bathe
breathe
brother
other
smooth

clothes /kloʊðz/

father /ˈfaðər/

feather /ˈfɛðər/

leather /ˈlɛðər/

mother /ˈmʌðər/

weather /ˈwɛðər/

Part 5B: Write and read

1. Mo___er ba___es ___e o___er bro___er.

2. Brea___e ano___er fea___er toge___er.

3. Fa___er's smoo___ lea___er wea___er clo___es.

Part 6: Fun review

Unscramble the words, write sentences

1. H O E S S these shoes
   [he / store]

2. R S H T S O H
   [where / she]

3. I S T R S H
   [you / mall]

4. E S E S R S D
   [where / I]

1. He bought these shoes at the store.
2. Where did she buy _____?
3. _____
4. _____

Winner's Tip!
- "at the" <u>place</u>
- "in" <u>country name</u>
- "online"

those
[she / store]

5. n e s s j a
6. o s c s k   [where / you]
7. v o l e s g e   [they / Japan]
8. s t o o b   [where / he]

5. _____
6. _____
7. _____
8. _____

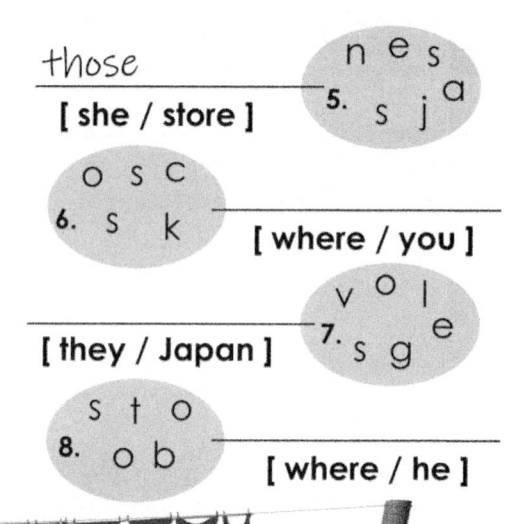

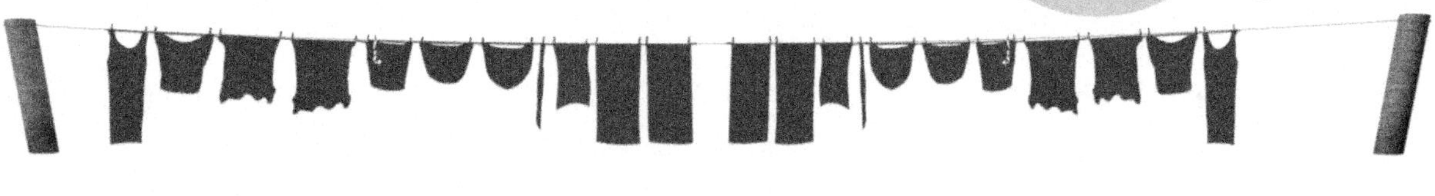

114

Lesson 19: More places

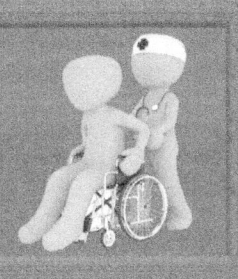

mais lugares

Part 1A: Learn the words

1. the **bus stop**
   ponto de ônibus
2. the **clinic**
   clínica
3. the **factory**
   fábrica
4. the **fire station**
   corpo de bombeiros
5. the **hospital**
   hospital
6. the **library**
   biblioteca
7. the **office**
   escritório
8. the **police station**
   delegacia de polícia
9. the **school**
   escola
10. the **train station**
    estação de trem

⭐ Practice speaking: "_Fábrica_" means "_factory_"! ⭐

Part 1B: Write the words

Write the missing letters!   Write x 1   Write x 2

1. b_s _t_p
2. _l_n_c
3. f_c_o_y
4. _i_e _t_t_o_
5. h_s_i_a_
6. _i_r_r_
7. o_f_c_
8. _o_i_e s_a_i_n
9. s_h_o_
10. _r_i_ s_a_i_n

115

Part 2A: Ask a question

Where will you go tomorrow?

✓ Tomorrow, I'll go to the library. I won't go to the school.

Where will he go later?

✓ Later, he'll go to the clinic. He won't go to the office.

⭐ **Winner's Tip!** won't = will not
Use: later, tomorrow, next week, next month

Part 2B: Fill in the blanks

1. Where _____ you go _____?
   Next week, I'll go to _____. I won't go to _____.

2. _____ will _____ go _____?
   Later, _____ go to _____. He won't go to the office.

3. _____ _____ she _____ _____?
   Tomorrow, she'll go to _____. She won't go to _____.

4. _____ _____ we _____ _____?
   Next month, we'll go to _____. We won't go to _____.

Part 3A: Yes / No questions

Will you go to the police station next week?

✓ **Yes, I will. I'll go** there next week.
✗ **No, I won't. I won't go** there next week.

Will they go to the train station next month?

✓ **Yes, they will. They'll go** there next month.
✗ **No, they won't. They won't go** there next month.

⭐ **Winner's Tip!** I'll / you'll / he'll / she'll / it'll / we'll / they'll

Part 3B: Fill in the blanks

1. Will _____ go _____ the bus stop tomorrow?
   Yes, he _____. He'll _____ there _____.

2. _____ she _____ to _____ next week?
   No, she _____. _____ won't go there _____.

3. _____ _____ go to _____ next month?
   No, we _____. We won't go _____ _____.

4. Will _____ _____ to _____ later?
   Yes, they _____. _____ go _____ _____.

Part 4A: Verb of the day

go / goes – went – going – gone (ir)

Every afternoon, we <u>go</u> to the train station.

He usually <u>goes</u> to the library with a friend.

Yesterday, we all <u>went</u> to the bus stop.

She is <u>going</u> to the fire station right now.

We have never <u>gone</u> to the factory before.

Part 4B: Verb Practice

1. Every morning, we _____ to the school very early.
2. On Mondays, she _____ to the swimming pool.
3. Every summer, he _____ to the zoo with friends.
4. Last week, I _____ to the fruit market for pears.
5. Yesterday, we _____ to the new department store.
6. Last year, she _____ to Australia for a trip.
7. Right now, I am _____ to the toy store for a doll.
8. We are _____ to the train station right now.
9. She has never _____ South Africa before.
10. We have _____ to many places in this big city.

Part 5A: Phonics Practice

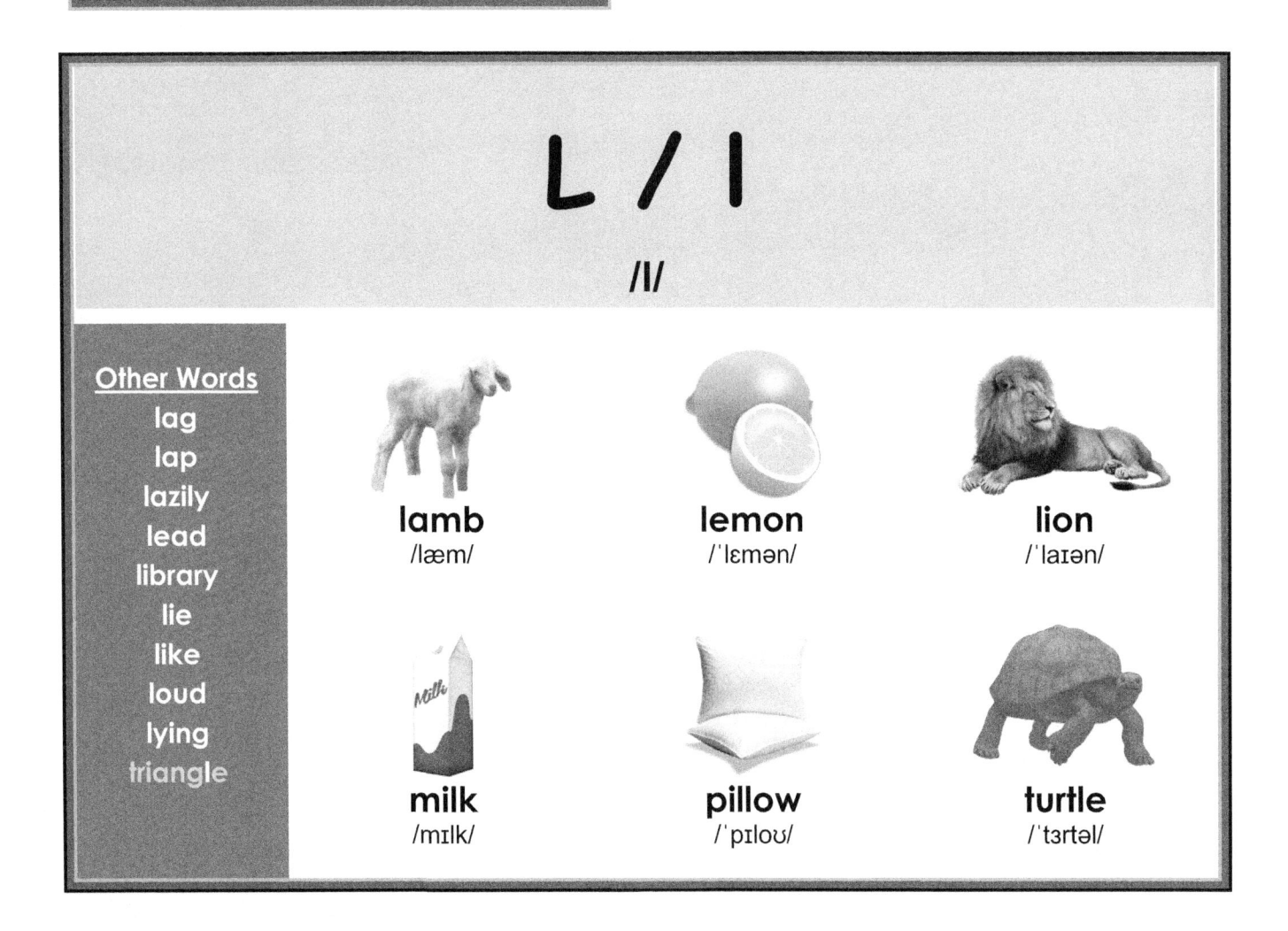

L / l
/l/

Other Words
lag
lap
lazily
lead
library
lie
like
loud
lying
triangle

lamb /læm/

lemon /ˈlɛmən/

lion /ˈlaɪən/

milk /mɪlk/

pillow /ˈpɪloʊ/

turtle /ˈtɜrtəl/

Part 5B: Write and read

1. __oud __ions __ead __agging __ambs.

2. Triang__e __ibrary pi__ows __ie __azi__y.

3. __ying turt__es __ike __apping __emon mi__k.

Part 6: Fun review

Write the answers

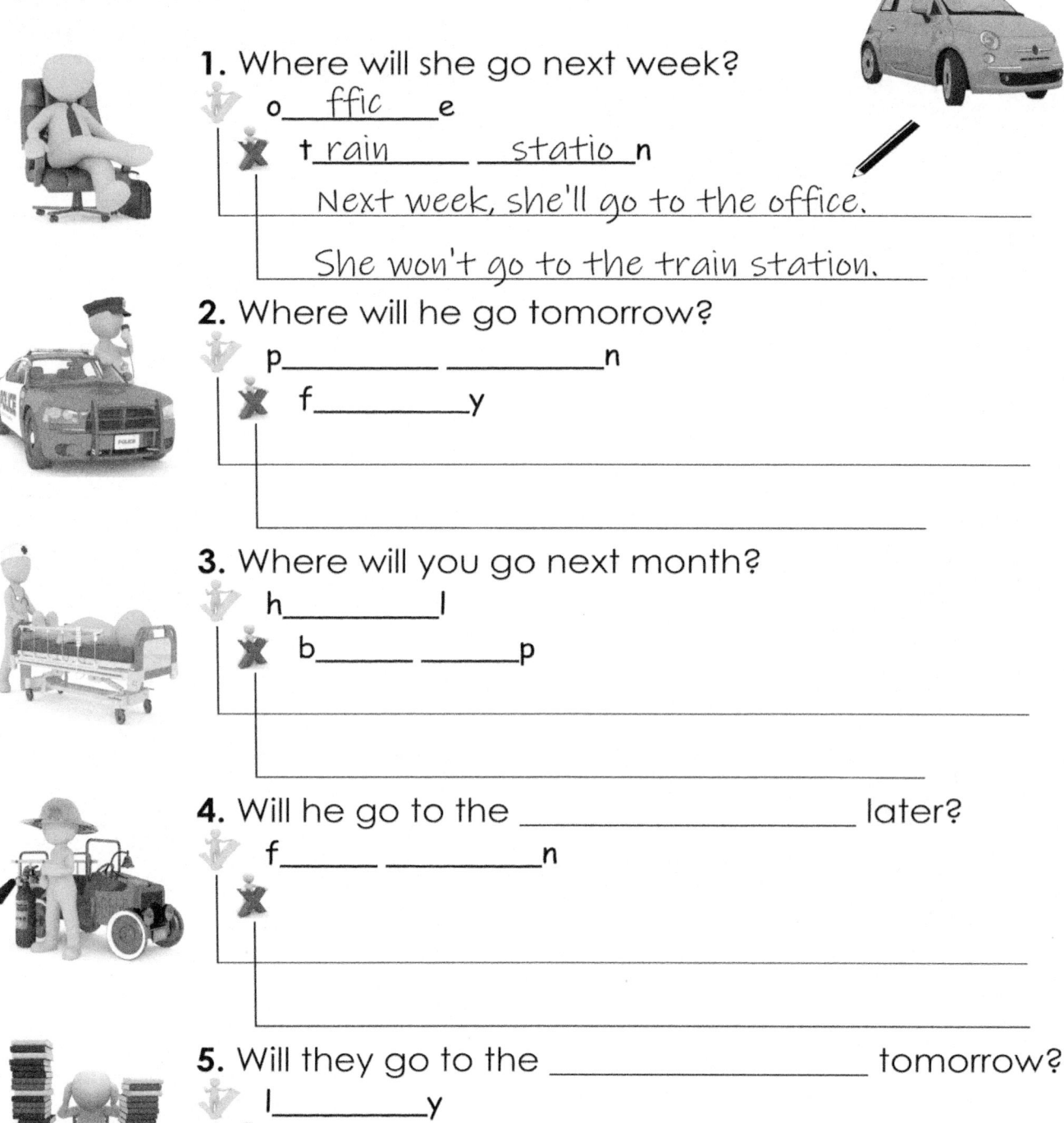

1. Where will she go next week?
   ✓ o__ffic__e
   ✗ t_rain_ _statio_n
   Next week, she'll go to the office.
   She won't go to the train station.

2. Where will he go tomorrow?
   ✓ p_____ _____n
   ✗ f_____y
   _____
   _____

3. Where will you go next month?
   ✓ h_____l
   ✗ b_____ _____p
   _____
   _____

4. Will he go to the _____ later?
   ✓ f_____ _____n
   ✗
   _____
   _____

5. Will they go to the _____ tomorrow?
   ✓ l_____y
   ✗
   _____
   _____

120

Lesson 20: The weather

o tempo

Part 1A: Learn the words

1. **cloudy**
   nublado
2. **cold**
   frio
3. **cool**
   fresco
4. **freezing**
   congelando
5. **hot**
   muito quente
6. **rainy**
   chuvoso
7. **snowy**
   nevado
8. **sunny**
   ensolarado
9. **warm**
   caloroso
10. **windy**
    ventoso

⭐ Practice speaking: "_Ensolarado_" is "_sunny_" in English! ⭐

Part 1B: Write the words

Write the missing letters!   Write x 1   Write x 2

1. c__o__d__
2. __o__d
3. c__o__
4. __r__e__i__g
5. __o__
6. r__i__y
7. __n__w__
8. s__n__y
9. __a__m
10. w__n__y

Part 2A: Ask a question

What will the weather be like <u>on Monday</u>?

✓ **On Monday,** the weather will be <u>cold</u>. It won't be <u>hot</u>.

What will the weather be like <u>next week</u>?

✓ **Next week,** it will be <u>rainy</u>. It won't be <u>windy</u>.

⭐ **Winner's Tip!** on...Monday, Tuesday, Wednesday, Thursday, Friday, Saturday, Sunday

Part 2B: Fill in the blanks

1. What _____ the weather be like _____?
   On Tuesday, _____ will be cool. It won't be _____.

2. _____ will the weather be _____ _____?
   Tomorrow, _____ will be _____. It won't be sunny.

3. What _____ the _____ be like _____?
   Next week, it _____ be windy. It won't be _____.

4. _____ _____ the _____ be like _____?
   On Friday, it will be _____. It _____ be _____.

122

Part 3A: Yes / No questions

Will the weather be <u>hot</u> <u>on Thursday</u>?

✓ **Yes, it will be. The weather will be** hot on Thursday.
✗ **No, it won't be. It won't be** hot **that day.**

Will the weather be <u>windy</u> <u>tomorrow</u>?

✓ **Yes, it will be. The weather will be** windy tomorrow.
✗ **No, it won't be. It won't be** windy tomorrow.

⭐ **Winner's Tip!** Answer with "it" for "the weather"

Part 3B: Fill in the blanks

1. _____ the _____ be snowy _____?
   Yes, _____ will be. It _____ be snowy on Monday.

2. Will _____ _____ be rainy tomorrow?
   No, it _____ be. It won't be _____ that day.

3. _____ the _____ be warm _____?
   No, it _____ be. It won't be _____ next week.

4. _____ the _____ be _____ on Thursday?
   _____, it will be. It _____ be sunny that day.

Part 4A: Verb of the day

feel / feels – felt – feeling – felt (sentir)

Often, I <u>feel</u> cold when I sleep at night.

Every summer, it <u>feels</u> very hot outside.

Yesterday, we <u>felt</u> tired after our classes.

She is <u>feeling</u> a little sick after she fell.

I have never <u>felt</u> so happy before!

Part 4B: Verb Practice

1. Every time I take a trip, I _____ very excited.
2. Each time he's sick, he _____ really uncomfortable.
3. On Fridays, she _____ quite tired after work.
4. Last Tuesday, we _____ hot in the sunny weather.
5. Yesterday, I _____ the wind blowing in my hair.
6. This morning, he _____ awake after he had coffee.
7. She is _____ sad now because the weekend is done.
8. We are _____ hot after exercising at the gym.
9. He has never _____ freezing weather before.
10. I have _____ really cold since this morning.

Part 5A: Phonics Practice

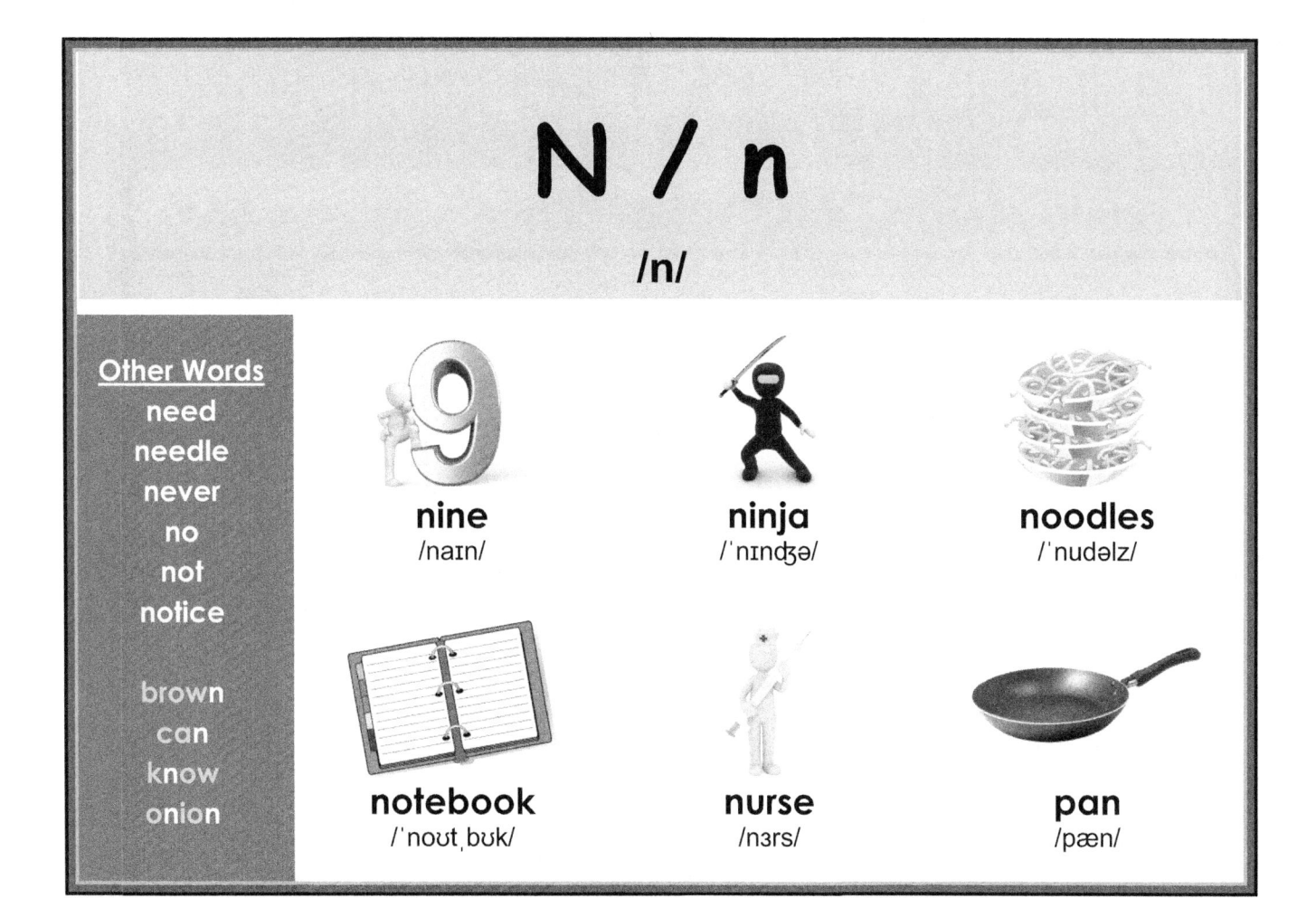

N / n
/n/

Other Words
need
needle
never
no
not
notice

brown
can
know
onion

nine
/naɪn/

ninja
/ˈnɪndʒə/

noodles
/ˈnudəlz/

notebook
/ˈnoʊtˌbʊk/

nurse
/nɜrs/

pan
/pæn/

Part 5B: Write and read

1. __i__e __i__jas __eed __o __otebooks.

2. __urses k__ow __eedles __ot __oodles.

3. __otice pa__ o__io__ ca__ __ever brow__.

Part 6: Fun review

Check the weather and write the answers

Sun	Mon	Tues	Wed	Thur	Fri	Sat
		1	2	3	4	5
6	7	8	9	10	11	12

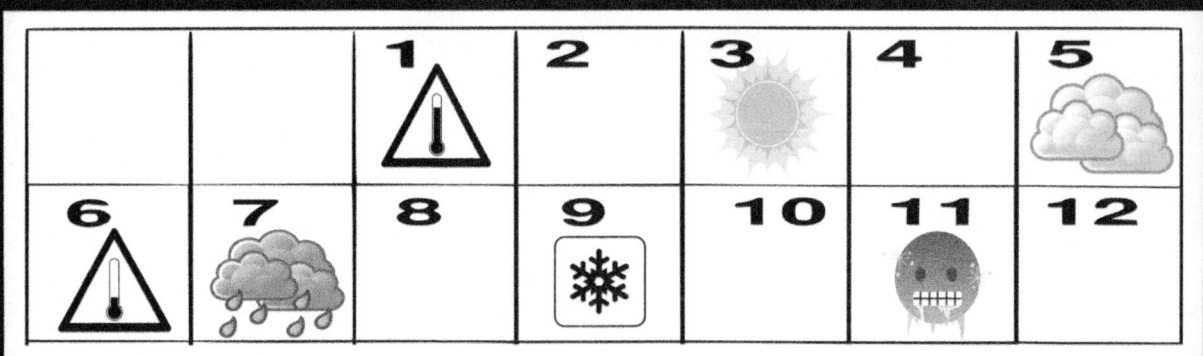

1. What will the weather be like on Tuesday?
   <u>On Tuesday, the weather will be hot. It won't be windy.</u>

2. What will the weather be like on Thursday?
   _____

3. What will the weather be like on Saturday?
   _____

4. What will the weather be like on Monday?
   _____

5. Will the weather be cold on Sunday?
   _____

6. Will the weather be warm on Wednesday?
   _____

7. Will the weather be freezing on Friday?
   _____

TEST 4: Lessons 16 - 20

Write the correct answer next to the letter "A"

A: ___ 1. Where did you buy _____ pants? I bought _____ online.
a) those / them
b) these / they
c) these / it
d) them / those

A: ___ 2. Where will he _____ later? Later, _____ go to the fire station.
a) goes / he will
b) go / he's
c) go / he'll
d) going / he

A: ___ 3. Will the weather _____ snowy on Friday? No, it _____ be.
a) is / isn't
b) are / will
c) being / will not
d) be / won't

A: ___ 4. What kind of meat _____ he _____ for lunch? He ate ham for lunch.
a) do / eat
b) is / ate
c) did / eat
d) did / ate

A: ___ 5. She always _____ some _____ in the nurse's office.
a) put / marker
b) puts / markers
c) puts / marker
d) putting / markers

A: ___ 6. What _____ the weather _____ like next week?
a) will / be
b) is / being
c) will / being
d) is / be

A: ___ 7. Did you eat salami for _____? Yes, I _____. I ate salami for a snack.
a) snack / did
b) a snack / did
c) lunch / ate
d) a snack / ate

A: ___ 8. Did he _____ a coach in the gym yesterday? Yes, he _____.
a) saw / saw
b) see / saw
c) sees / does
d) see / did

A: ___ 9. Did we buy _____ jeans in Australia? No, we _____.
a) these / don't
b) these / didn't
c) those / haven't
d) those / didn't buy

127

A: ___ **10.** Will you go to the office next week? Yes, I ____. ____ go there then.
a) go / I won't **b)** going / I
c) will / I'll **d)** will / I

A: ___ **11.** Last weekend, he _____ me _____ boots.
a) lends / those **b)** lending / some
c) lent / these **d)** lend / any

A: ___ **12.** Where did they _____ the principal last month?
Last month, they _____ the principal in the computer lab.
a) see / seeing **b)** saw / saw
c) see / saw **d)** saw / seeing

A: ___ **13.** Last night, _____ _____ dinner late at night with his family.
a) we / eating **b)** he / eats
c) you / eat **d)** they / ate

A: ___ **14.** _____ usually _____ to the train station with her friends.
a) He / go **b)** She / goes
c) They / going **d)** She / going

A: ___ **15.** He _____ _____ really cold in this winter weather.
a) is / feels **b)** is / feeling
c) has / feel **d)** has / feeling

A: ___ **16.** Did she _____ shrimp for dinner? No, she _____.
a) eat / didn't **b)** eat / didn't eat
c) have / doesn't **d)** ate / don't

A: ___ **17.** Yesterday, we ____ the teacher ____ the pencil in the classroom.
a) saw / put **b)** seeing / puts
c) see / putting **d)** seen / put

A: ___ **18.** Will the _____ be _____ next week?
a) windy / weather **b)** cloudy / warm
c) weather / freezing **d)** weather / freeze

Answers on page 129

TEST ANSWERS

Test 1
1) c 2) a 3) b 4) a 5) d 6) c 7) d 8) b 9) d 10) a 11) c 12) c 13) b 14) d 15) c 16) a 17) b 18) d

Test 2
1) b 2) d 3) a 4) d 5) c 6) b 7) c 8) c 9) a 10) b 11) d 12) d 13) c 14) a 15) d 16) b 17) c 18) a

Test 3
1) d 2) b 3) c 4) b 5) a 6) d 7) a 8) a 9) c 10) d 11) a 12) b 13) a 14) c 15) c 16) d 17) b 18) b

Test 4
1) a 2) c 3) d 4) c 5) b 6) a 7) b 8) d 9) b 10) c 11) c 12) c 13) d 14) b 15) b 16) a 17) a 18) c

Winner!

Printed in Great Britain
by Amazon